THE NATION'S
FAVOURITE
CHILDREN'S POEMS

Also available from BBC Worldwide:

The Nation's Favourite Poems
ISBN: 0 563 38782 3
ISBN: 0 563 38487 5 (hardback gift edition)

The Nation's Favourite Love Poems
ISBN: 0 563 38378 X
ISBN: 0 563 38432 8 (hardback gift edition)

The Nation's Favourite Comic Poems
ISBN: 0 563 38451 4

The Nation's Favourite Twentieth Century Poems
ISBN: 0 563 55143 7

The Nation's Favourite Shakespeare
ISBN: 0 563 55142 9

The Nation's Favourite Poems of Childhood
ISBN: 0 563 55184 4

The Nation's Favourite Poems of Journeys
ISBN: 0 563 53715 9

The Nation's Favourite Animal Poems
ISBN: 0 563 53780 9

Audio cassettes available from BBC Radio Collection:

The Nation's Favourite Poems
ISBN: 0 563 38987 7

The Nation's Favourite Love Poems
ISBN: 0 563 38279 1

The Nation's Favourite Comic Poems
ISBN: 0 563 55850 4

The Nation's Favourite Shakespeare
ISBN: 0 563 55331 6

The Nation's Favourite Lakeland Poems
ISBN: 0 563 55293 X

The Nation's Favourite Poems of Childhood
ISBN: 0 563 47727 X

The above titles are also available on CD

THE NATION'S
FAVOURITE
CHILDREN'S POEMS

— ◇ —

FOREWORD BY
SPIKE MILLIGAN

Published in 2001 by BBC Books, an imprint of Ebury Publishing
A Random House Group Company

The Random House Group Limited Reg. No. 954009

Addresses for companies within the Random House Group can be found at
www.randomhouse.co.uk

15

Edited and compiled by Alex Warwick
Compilation © BBC Worldwide 2001
Poems © individual copyright holders

Illustrations by Josephine Sumner

ISBN 978 0 563 53774 8

Printed and bound by CPI Group
(UK) Ltd, Croydon, CR0 4YY

THE POETRY SOCIETY

The Poetry Society has been promoting poets and poetry in Britain since 1909.
A membership organisation open to all, it publishes Britain's leading poetry
magazine, *Poetry Review*, runs the National Poetry Competition, has a
lively education programme and offers advice and information on reading and
writing poetry. For further information telephone 020 7420 9880 or email
info@poetrysoc.com
www.poetrysoc.com

The Random House Group Limited supports The Forest Stewardship Council
(FSC®), the leading international forest certification organisation. Our books
carrying the FSC label are printed on FSC® certified paper. FSC is the only fore
certification scheme endorsed by the leading environmental organisations,
including Greenpeace. Our paper procurement policy can be found at
www.randomhouse.co.uk/environment

MIX
Paper from
responsible sources
FSC® C016897

CONTENTS

— ◇ —

'Cats, you're aware, can repose in a chair,
Chickens can roost upon rails;
Puppies are able to sleep in a stable,
And oysters can slumber in pails'

'My little sister was truly awful,
She was really shocking,
She put the budgie in the fridge
And slugs in Mummy's stocking.'

5

– Contents –

'There, in the night, where none can spy,
All in my hunter's camp I lie,
And play at books that I have read
Till it is time to go to bed.'

– Contents –

> *'Belinda lived in a little white house,*
> *With a little black kitten and a little gray mouse,*
> *And a little yellow dog and a little red wagon,*
> *And a realio, trulio, little pet dragon.'*

> *'To understand the ways*
> *of alien beings is hard,*
> *and I've never worked it out*
> *why they landed in my backyard.'*

– Contents –

'The night will never stay,
The night will still go by,
Though with a million stars
You pin it to the sky'

'What a shame you can't buy
tokens of time, save them up
and lengthen the good days'

FOREWORD BY SPIKE MILLIGAN

— ◇ —

I have been asked by the BBC to write a foreword for *The Nation's Favourite Children's Poems* book. I can't believe and never would have thought, all those years ago (I've just realised it's nearly 50 years ago), when I was telling my children bedtime stories and making up rhymes such as 'On the Ning Nang Nong' to make them laugh, that I would be writing a foreword for all these wonderful children's poems.

This book is for children whatever their age. I myself would draw the line at 97 years of age. If they survive over that they must be on something that the NHS is dispensing like longevity tablets, which are a mixture of monkey glands and diddledums. I can't take any credit for any of this; believe me, I have tried to get them at every bank in England but I have failed, so that's that then.

I myself dote on children and if you look closely you will find that most children are covered all over in dote marks. Don't worry: Persil will remove these dote marks and leave them smelling fresh – fresh dote marks. So please don't dote on children; it leaves them covered in marks – dote marks. I wish all you children a lovely life. I hope none of you in your lifetime gets leprosy.

Now please don't bother me anymore – I'm busy washing off dote marks. So goodbye and stinky poo to all of you.

THE TOP-TEN CHILDREN'S POEMS

The BBC celebrated National Poetry Day 2001 by launching a poll to find the nation's favourite children's poem – here are the results.

1 The Owl and the Pussy-Cat
Edward Lear

2 Matilda
Hilaire Belloc

3 Don't
Michael Rosen

4 Jabberwocky
Lewis Carroll

5 On the Ning Nang Nong
Spike Milligan

6 Talking Turkeys!!
Benjamin Zephaniah

7 Macavity, The Mystery Cat
T.S. Eliot

8 The King's Breakfast
A.A. Milne

9 Please Mrs Butler
Allan Ahlberg

10 'Down Vith Children! Do Them In!' from *The Witches*
Roald Dahl

'Cats, you're aware, can repose in a chair,
Chickens can roost upon rails;
Puppies are able to sleep in a stable,
And oysters can slumber in pails'

from 'The Camel's Complaint'

RICHARD DIGANCE (1949–)

THE BEAR

When the Bear held a Fancy Dress Party,
just about everyone went.
Each animal went as another.
Well, at least that was the intent.

The Bat and Bull went as a Cricket
and the Bison went as a Bath.
The Viper sat on the Hyena's head
and they went as a laughing Giraffe.

The Eagle went as a Birdie
and the Birdie went as a Parr.
(A Parr is an under-aged Salmon,
in case you don't know what they are.)

The Panda turned up like a Penguin,
though he hadn't quite mastered the walk.
No one could tell the difference
when the Butterfly dressed like a Stork.

The Hedgehog turned up as a Buffalo
(Hedgehogs not being that bright),
but everyone said that he'd tried very hard
and he had an enjoyable night.

He almost came second for trying,
but it went to the Hippo instead.
He dressed up as a fairy-tale Unicorn,
with an ice-cream stuck on his head.

The Oyster, disguised as a jewellery box,
sang when his shell opened up.
A good try by Oyster but not good enough
to take home the Fancy Dress Cup.

the Skunk was most unconvincing,
sprinting in like a Gazelle.
It's hard for a Skunk to be anything else,
when they have that distinctive smell.

It was time to declare the Cup winner
and first place went to the Cat,
who covered his tail with red rubber
and hung from a tree like a Bat.

T. S. ELIOT (1888–1965)

MR MISTOFFELEES

You ought to know Mr Mistoffelees!
The Original Conjuring Cat—
(There can be no doubt about that).
Please listen to me and don't scoff. All his
Inventions are off his own bat.
There's no such Cat in the metropolis;
He holds all the patent monopolies
For performing surprising illusions
And creating eccentric confusions.
    At prestidigitation
    And at legerdemain
    He'll defy examination
    And deceive you again.
The greatest magicians have something to learn
From Mr Mistoffelees' Conjuring Turn.
Presto!
    Away we go!
    And we all say: OH!
    Well I never!
    Was there ever
    A Cat so clever
    As Magical Mr Mistoffelees!

He is quiet and small, he is black
From his ears to the top of his tail;
He can creep through the tiniest crack
He can walk on the narrowest rail.
He can pick any card from a pack,
He is equally cunning with dice;
He is always deceiving you into believing
That he's only hunting for mice.
    He can play any trick with a cork
    Or a spoon and a bit of fish-paste;
    If you look for a knife or a fork

And you think it is merely misplaced—
You have seen it one moment, and then it is *gawn*!
But you'll find it next week lying out on the lawn.
    And we all say: OH!
    Well I never!
    Was there ever
    A Cat so clever
    As Magical Mr Mistoffelees!

His manner is vague and aloof,
You would think there was nobody shyer—
But his voice has been heard on the roof
When he was curled up by the fire.
And he's sometimes been heard by the fire
When he was about on the roof—
(At least we all *heard* that somebody purred)
Which is incontestable proof
    Of his singular magical powers:
    And I have known the family to call
    Him in from the garden for hours,
    While he was asleep in the hall.
And not long ago this phenomenal Cat
Produced *seven kittens* right out of a hat!
    And we all said: OH!
    Well I never!
    Did you ever
    Know a Cat so clever
    As Magical Mr Mistoffelees!

A. E. HOUSMAN (1859–1936)

THE AFRICAN LION

To meet a bad lad on the African waste
    Is a thing that a lion enjoys;
But he rightly and strongly objects to the taste
    Of good and uneatable boys.

When he bites off a piece of a boy of that sort
    He spits it right out of his mouth,
And retires with a loud and dissatisfied snort
    To the east, or the west, or the south.

So lads of good habits, on coming across
    A lion, need feel no alarm,
For they know they are sure to escape with the loss
    Of a leg, or a head, or an arm.

ROGER MCGOUGH (1937–)

THE CATS' PROTECTION LEAGUE

Midnight. A knock at the door.
Open it? Better had.
Three heavy cats, mean and bad.

They offer protection. I ask, 'What for?'
The Boss-cat snarls, 'You know the score.
Listen man and listen good

If you wanna stay in the neighbourhood,
Pay your dues or the toms will call
And wail each night on the backyard wall.

Mangle the flowers, and as for the lawn
A smelly minefield awaits you at dawn.'
These guys meant business without a doubt

Three cans of tuna, I handed them out.
They then disappeared like bats into hell
Those bad, bad cats from the CPL.

MARY ANN HOBERMAN (1930–)

WHALE

A whale is stout about the middle,
He is stout about the ends,
& so is all his family
& so are all his friends.

He's pleased that he's enormous,
He's happy he weighs tons,
& so are all his daughters
& so are all his sons.

He eats when he is hungry
Each kind of food he wants,
& so do all his uncles
& so do all his aunts.

He doesn't mind his blubber,
He doesn't mind his creases,
& neither do his nephews
& neither do his nieces.

You may find him chubby,
You may find him fat,
But he would disagree with you:
He likes himself like that.

CHARLES CAUSLEY (1917–)

I SAW A JOLLY HUNTER

I saw a jolly hunter
  With a jolly gun
Walking in the country
  In the jolly sun.

In the jolly meadow
  Sat a jolly hare.
Saw the jolly hunter.
  Took jolly care.

Hunter jolly eager—
  Sight of jolly prey.
Forgot gun pointing
  Wrong jolly way.

Jolly hunter jolly head
  Over heels gone.
Jolly old safety catch
  Not jolly on.

Bang went the jolly gun.
  Hunter jolly dead.
Jolly hare got clean away.
  Jolly good, I said.

JOHN AGARD (1949–)

DON'T CALL ALLIGATOR LONG-MOUTH TILL YOU CROSS RIVER

Call alligator long-mouth
call alligator saw-mouth
call alligator pushy-mouth
call alligator scissors-mouth
call alligator raggedy-mouth
call alligator bumpy-bum
call alligator all dem rude word
but better wait
                till you cross river.

HILAIRE BELLOC (1870–1953)

THE MICROBE

The Microbe is so very small
You cannot make him out at all,
But many sanguine people hope
To see him through a microscope.
His jointed tongue that lies beneath
A hundred curious rows of teeth;
His seven tufted tails with lots
Of lovely pink and purple spots,
On each of which a pattern stands,
Composed of forty separate bands;
His eyebrows of a tender green;
All these have never yet been seen—
But Scientists, who ought to know,
Assure us that they must be so . . .
Oh! let us never, never doubt
What nobody is sure about!

SPIKE MILLIGAN (1918–)

TODAY I SAW A LITTLE WORM

Today I saw a little worm
Wriggling on his belly.
Perhaps he'd like to come inside
And see what's on the Telly.

HILAIRE BELLOC (1870–1953)

THE FROG

Be kind and tender to the Frog,
    And do not call him names,
As 'Slimy skin', or 'Polly-wog',
    Or likewise 'Ugly James',
Or 'Gape-a-grin', or 'Toad-gone-wrong',
    Or 'Billy Bandy-knees':
The Frog is justly sensitive
    To epithets like these.
No animal will more repay
    A treatment kind and fair;
At least so lonely people say
Who keep a frog (and, by the way,
    They are extremely rare).

KENNETH GRAHAME (1859–1932)

'SONG OF MR TOAD'
from THE WIND IN THE WILLOWS

The world has held great Heroes,
    As history-books have showed;
But never a name to go down to fame
    Compared with that of Toad!

The clever men at Oxford
    Know all that there is to be knowed.
But they none of them know one half as much
    As intelligent Mr Toad!

The animals sat in the Ark and cried,
    Their tears in torrents flowed.
Who was it said, 'There's land ahead'?
    Encouraging Mr Toad!

The Army all saluted
    As they marched along the road,
Was it the King? Or Kitchener?
    No. It was Mr Toad!

The Queen and her Ladies-in-waiting
    Sat in the window and sewed.
She cried, 'Look! who's that *handsome* man?'
    They answered, 'Mr Toad.'

G. K. CHESTERTON (1874–1936)

TRIOLET

I wish I were a jellyfish
That cannot fall downstairs:
Of all the things I wish to wish
I wish I were a jellyfish
That hasn't any cares,
And doesn't even have to wish
'I wish I were a jellyfish
That cannot fall downstairs.'

JOHN CLARE (1793–1864)

LITTLE TROTTY WAGTAIL

Little trotty wagtail he went in the rain
And tittering tottering sideways he near got straight again
He stooped to get a worm and look'd up to catch a fly
And then he flew away e're his feathers they were dry

Little trotty wagtail he waddled in the mud
And left his little foot marks trample where he would
He waddled in the water pudge and waggle went his tail
And chirrupt up his wings to dry upon the garden rail

Little trotty wagtail you nimble all about
And in the dimpling water pudge you waddle in and out
Your home is nigh at hand and in the warm pigsty
So little Master Wagtail I'll bid you a 'Good bye'

BENJAMIN ZEPHANIAH (1958–)

TALKING TURKEYS!!

Be nice to yu turkeys dis christmas
Cos turkeys jus wanna hav fun
Turkeys are cool, turkeys are wicked
An every turkey has a Mum.
Be nice to yu turkeys dis christmas.
Don't eat it, keep it alive,
It could be yu mate and not on yu plate
Say, Yo! Turkey I'm on your side.

I got lots of friends who are turkeys
An all of dem fear christmas time,
Dey wanna enjoy it, dey say humans destroyed it
An humans are out of dere mind,
Yeah, I got lots of friends who are turkeys
Dey all hav a right to a life,
Not to be caged up an genetically made up
By any farmer an his wife.

Turkeys jus wanna play reggae
Turkeys jus wanna hip-hop
Can yu imagine a nice young turkey saying,
'I cannot wait for de chop'?
Turkeys like getting presents, dey wanna watch christmas TV,
Turkeys hav brains an turkeys feel pain
In many ways like you an me.

I once knew a turkey called
Turkey
He said 'Benji explain to me please,
Who put de turkey in christmas
An what happens to chritsmas trees?'
I said, 'I am not too sure turkey
But it's nothing to do wid Christ Mass
Humans get greedy an waste more dan need be
An business men mek loadsa cash.'

Be nice to yu turkey dis christmas
Invite dem indoors fe sum greens
Let dem eat cake an let dem partake
In a plate of organic grown beans,
Be nice to yu turkey dis christmas
An spare dem de cut of de knife,
Join Turkeys United an dey'll be delighted
An yu will mek new friends 'FOR LIFE'.

CHARLES CAUSLEY (1917–)

OUT IN THE DESERT

Out in the desert lies the sphinx
It never eats and it never drinx
Its body quite solid without any chinx
And when the sky's all purple and pinx
(As if it was painted with coloured inx)
And the sun it ever so swiftly sinx
Behind the hills in a couple of twinx
You may hear (if you're lucky) a bell that clinx
And also tolls and also tinx
And they say at the very same sound the sphinx
It sometimes smiles and it sometimes winx:

But nobody knows just what it thinx.

LEWIS CARROLL (1832–98)

THE MOUSE'S TALE

'Fury said to
a mouse, That
he met in the
house, "Let
us both go
to law: *I*
will prose-
cute *you*. —
Come, I'll
take no de-
nial: We
must have
the trial;
For really
this morn-
ing I've
nothing
to do."
Said the
mouse to
the cur,
"Such a
trial, dear
sir, With
no jury
or judge,
would
be wast-
ing our
breath."
"I'll be
judge,
I'll be
jury,"
said
cun-
ning
old
Fury:
"I'll
try
the
whole
cause,
and
con-
demn
you to
death."'

CHARLES E. CARRYL (1841–1920)

THE CAMEL'S COMPLAINT

Canary-birds feed on sugar and seed,
    Parrots have crackers to crunch;
And as for the poodles, they tell me the noodles
    Have chicken and cream for their lunch.
    But there's never a question
    About *my* digestion—
    Anything does for me.

Cats, you're aware, can repose in a chair,
    Chickens can roost upon rails;
Puppies are able to sleep in a stable,
    And oysters can slumber in pails,
    But no one supposes
    A poor camel dozes—
    Any place does for me.

Lambs are enclosed where it's never exposed,
    Coops are constructed for hens;
Kittens are treated to houses well heated,
    And pigs are protected by pens.
    But a camel comes handy
    Wherever it's sandy—
    Anywhere does for me.

People would laugh if you rode a giraffe,
    Or mounted the back of an ox;
It's nobody's habit to ride on a rabbit,
    Or try to bestraddle a fox.
    But as for a camel, he's
    Ridden by families—
    Any load does for me.

A snake is as round as a hole in the ground,
   And weasels are wavy and sleek;
And no alligator could ever be straighter
   Than lizards that live in a creek.
   But a camel's all lumpy
   And bumpy and humpy—
   Any shape does for me.

KENNETH GRAHAME (1859–1932)

DUCKS' DITTY

All along the backwater,
Through the rushes tall,
Ducks are a-dabbling,
Up tails all!

Ducks' tails, drakes' tails,
Yellow feet a-quiver,
Yellow bills all out of sight
Busy in the river!

Slushy green undergrowth
Where the roach swim —
Here we keep our larder,
Cool and full and dim.

Every one for what he likes!
We like to be
Heads down, tails up,
Dabbling free!

High in the blue above
Swifts whirl and call —
We are down a-dabbling
Up tails all!

EUGENE FIELD (1850–95)

THE DUEL

The gingham dog and the calico cat
Side by side on the table sat;
'Twas half-past twelve, and (what do you think!)
Nor one nor t'other had slept a wink!
   The old Dutch clock and the Chinese plate
   Appeared to know so sure as fate
There was going to be a terrible spat.
   (*I wasn't there; I simply state
   What was told to me by the Chinese plate*!)

The gingham dog went 'bow-wow-wow!'
And the calico cat replied 'mee-ow!'
The air was littered, an hour or so,
With bits of gingham and calico,
   While the old Dutch clock in the chimney-place
   Up with its hands before its face,
For it always dreaded a family row!
   (*Now mind: I'm only telling you
   What the old Dutch clock declares is true*!)

The Chinese plate looked very blue,
And wailed, 'Oh, dear! what shall we do!'
But the gingham dog and the calico cat
Wallowed this way and tumbled that,
   Employing every tooth and claw
   In the awfullest way you ever saw—
And, oh! how the gingham and calico flew!
   (*Don't fancy I exaggerate—
   I got my news from the Chinese plate*!)

Next morning, where the two had sat
They found no trace of dog or cat;
And some folks think unto this day
That burglars stole that pair away!
      But the truth about the cat and pup
      Is this: they ate each other up!
      Now what do you really think of that!
      (The old Dutch clock it told me so,
      And that is how I came to know.)

MICHAEL FLANDERS (1922–75)

THE HIPPOPOTAMUS SONG

A bold Hippopotamus was standing one day
On the banks of the cool Shalimar.
He gazed at the bottom as it peacefully lay
By the light of the evening star.
Away on a hilltop sat combing her hair
His fair Hippopotamine maid;
The Hippopotamus was no ignoramus
And sang her this sweet serenade.

    Mud, Mud, glorious mud,
    Nothing quite like it for cooling the blood!
    So follow me, follow,
    Down to the hollow
    And there let us wallow
    In glorious mud!

The fair Hippopotama he aimed to entice
From her seat on that hilltop above,
As she hadn't got a ma to give her advice,
Came tiptoeing down to her love.
Like thunder the forest re-echoed the sound
Of the song that they sang as they met.
His inamorata adjusted her garter
And lifted her voice in duet.

    Mud, Mud, glorious mud,
    Nothing quite like it for cooling the blood!
    So follow me, follow,
    Down to the hollow
    And there let us wallow
    In glorious mud!

Now more Hippopotami began to convene
On the banks of that river so wide.
I wonder now what am I to say of the scene
That ensued by the Shalimar side?
They dived all at once with an ear-splitting splosh
Then rose to the surface again,
A regular army of Hippopotami
All singing this haunting refrain.

    Mud! Mud! Glorious mud!
    Nothing quite like it for cooling the blood.
    So follow me, follow,
    Down to the hollow
    And there let us wallow
    In glorious mud!

'My little sister was truly awful,
She was really shocking,
She put the budgie in the fridge
And slugs in Mummy's stocking.'

from 'The Trouble with My Sister'

A. A. MILNE (1882–1956)

US TWO

Wherever I am, there's always Pooh,
There's always Pooh and Me.
Whatever I do, he wants to do,
'Where are you going today?' says Pooh:
'Well, that's very odd 'cos I was too.
Let's go together,' says Pooh, says he.
'Let's go together,' says Pooh.

'What's twice eleven?' I said to Pooh,
('Twice what?' said Pooh to Me.)
'I *think* it ought to be twenty-two.'
'Just what I think myself,' said Pooh.
'It wasn't an easy sum to do,
But that's what it is,' said Pooh, said he.
'That's what it is,' said Pooh.

'Let's look for dragons,' I said to Pooh.
'Yes, let's,' said Pooh to Me.
We crossed the river and found a few—
'Yes, those are dragons all right,' said Pooh.
'As soon as I saw their beaks I knew.
That's what they are,' said Pooh, said he.
'That's what they are,' said Pooh.

'Let's frighten the dragons,' I said to Pooh.
'That's right,' said Pooh to Me.
'*I'm* not afraid,' I said to Pooh,
And I held his paw and I shouted, 'Shoo!
Silly old dragons!'—and off they flew.
'I wasn't afraid,' said Pooh, said he,
'I'm *never* afraid with you.'

So wherever I am, there's always Pooh,
There's always Pooh and Me.
'What would I do?' I said to Pooh,
'If it wasn't for you,' and Pooh said: 'True,
It isn't much fun for One, but Two
Can stick together,' says Pooh, says he.
'That's how it is,' says Pooh.

A. A. MILNE (1882–1956)

HAPPINESS

John had
Great Big
Waterproof
Boots on;
John had a
Great Big
Waterproof
Hat;
John had a
Great Big
Waterproof
Mackintosh—
And that
(Said John)
  Is
  That.

JAMES HOGG (1770–1835)

A BOY'S SONG

Where the pools are bright and deep,
Where the grey trout lies asleep,
Up the river and o'er the lea,
That's the way for Billy and me.

Where the blackbird sings the latest,
Where the hawthorn blooms the sweetest,
Where the nestlings chirp and flee,
That's the way for Billy and me.

Where the mowers mow the cleanest,
Where the hay lies thick and greenest;
There to trace the homeward bee,
That's the way for Billy and me.

Where the hazel bank is steepest,
Where the shadow falls the deepest,
Where the clustering nuts fall free,
That's the way for Billy and me.

Why the boys should drive away
Little sweet maidens from the play,
Or love to banter and fight so well,
That's the thing I never could tell.

But this I know, I love to play,
Through the meadow, among the hay;
Up the water and o'er the lea,
That's the way for Billy and me.

ROBERT LOUIS STEVENSON (1850–94)

GOOD AND BAD CHILDREN

Children, you are very little,
And your bones are very brittle;
If you would grow great and stately,
You must try to walk sedately.

You must still be bright and quiet,
And content with simple diet;
And remain, through all bewild'ring,
Innocent and honest children.

Happy hearts and happy faces,
Happy play in grassy places —
That was how, in ancient ages,
Children grew to kings and sages.

But the unkind and the unruly,
And the sort who eat unduly,
They must never hope for glory —
Theirs is quite a different story!

Cruel children, crying babies,
All grow up as geese and gabies,
Hated, as their age increases,
By their nephews and their nieces.

LEWIS CARROLL (1832–98)

A LULLABY

Speak roughly to your little boy,
    And beat him when he sneezes:
He only does it to annoy,
    Because he knows it teases.

    Wow! wow! wow!

I speak severely to my boy,
    I beat him when he sneezes;
For he can thoroughly enjoy
    The pepper when he pleases!

    Wow! wow! wow!

CHARLES E. CARRYL (1841–1920)

THE SLEEPY GIANT

My age is three hundred and seventy-two,
   And I think, with the deepest regret,
How I used to pick up and voraciously chew
   The dear little boys whom I met.

I've eaten them raw, in their holiday suits;
   I've eaten them curried with rice;
I've eaten them baked, in their jackets and boots,
   And found them exceedingly nice.

But now that my jaws are too weak for such fare,
   I think it exceedingly rude
To do such a thing, when I'm quite well aware
   Little boys do not like to be chewed.

And so I contentedly live upon eels,
   And try to do nothing amiss.
And I pass all the time I can spare from my meals
   In innocent slumber like this.

ROALD DAHL (1916–90)

'DOWN VITH CHILDREN! DO THEM IN!'
from THE WITCHES

'Down vith children! Do them in!
Boil their bones and fry their skin!
Bish them, sqvish them, bash them, mash them!
Brrreak them, shake them, slash them, smash them!
Offer chocs vith magic powder!
Say "Eat up!" then say it louder.
Crrram them full of sticky eats,
Send them home still guzzling sveets.
And in the morning little fools
Go marching off to separate schools.
A girl feels sick and goes all pale.
She yells, "Hey look! I've grrrown a tail!"
A boy who's standing next to her
Screams, "Help! I think I'm grrrowing fur!"
Another shouts, "Vee look like frrreaks!
There's viskers growing on our cheeks!"
A boy who vos extremely tall
Cries Out, 'Vot's wrong? I'm grrrowing small!"
Four tiny legs begin to sprrrout
From everybody rrround about.
And all at vunce, all in a trrrice,
There are no children! Only MICE!
In every school is mice galore
All rrrunning rrround the school-rrroom floor!
And all the poor demented teachers
Is yelling, "Hey, who are these crrreatures?"
They stand upon the desks and shout,
"Get out, you filthy mice! Get out!
Vill someone fetch some mouse-trrraps, please!
And don't forrrget to bring the cheese!"
Now mouse-trrraps come and every trrrap
Goes *snippy-snip* and *snappy-snap*.
The mouse-trrraps have a powerful spring,

The springs go *crack* and *snap* and *ping*!
Is lovely noise for us to hear!
Is music to a vitch's ear!
Dead mice is every place arrround,
Piled two feet deep upon the grrround,
Vith teachers searching left and rrright,
But not a single child in sight!
The teachers cry, "Vot's going on?
Oh vhere have all the children gone?
Is half-past nine and as a rrrule
They're never late as this for school!"
Poor teachers don't know vot to do.
Some sit and rrread, and just a few
Amuse themselves throughout the day
By sveeping all the mice avay.
AND ALL US VITCHES SHOUT HOORAY!'

BRIAN PATTEN (1946–)

THE TROUBLE WITH MY SISTER

My little sister was truly awful,
She was really shocking,
She put the budgie in the fridge
And slugs in Mummy's stocking.

She was really awful
But it was a load of fun
When she stole Uncle Wilbur's
Double-barrelled gun.

She aimed it at a pork pie
And blew it into bits,
She aimed it at a hamster
That was having fits.

She leapt up on the telly,
She pirouetted on the cat,
She gargled with some jelly
And spat in Grandad's hat.

She ran down the hallway,
She ran across the road,
She dug up lots of earth-worms
And caught a squirming toad.

She put them in a large pot
And she began to stir.
She added a pint of bat's blood
And some rabbit fur.

She leapt up on the Hoover,
Around the room she went.
Once she had a turned-up nose
But now her nose is bent.

I like my little sister,
There is really just one hitch,
I think my little sister
Has become a little witch.

TED HUGHES (1930–98)

MY OTHER GRANNY

My Granny is an Octopus
    At the bottom of the sea,
And when she comes to supper
    She brings her family.

She chooses a wild wet windy night
    When the world rolls blind
As a boulder in the night-sea surf,
    And her family troops behind.

The sea-smell enters with them
    As they sidle and slither and spill
With their huge eyes and their tiny eyes
    And a dripping ocean-chill.

Some of her cousins are lobsters
    Some floppy jelly fish—
What would you be if your family tree
    Grew out of such a dish?

Her brothers are crabs jointed and knobbed
    With little pinhead eyes,
Their pincers crack the biscuits
    And they bubble joyful cries.

Crayfish the size of ponies
    Creak as they sip their milk.
My father stares in horror
    At my mother's secret ilk.

They wave long whiplash antennae,
    They sizzle and they squirt—
We smile and waggle our fingers back
    Or grandma would be hurt.

'What's new, Ma?' my father asks,
    'Down in the marvellous deep?'
Her face swells up, her eyes bulge huge
    And she begins to weep.

She knots her sucker tentacles
    And gapes like a nestling bird,
And her eyes flash, changing stations,
    As she attempts a WORD

Then out of her eyes there brim two drops
    That plop into her saucer—
And that is all she manages,
    And my Dad knows he can't force her.

And when they've gone, my ocean-folk,
    No man could prove they came—
For the sea-tears in her saucer
    And a man's tears are the same.

GRACE NICHOLS (1950–)

GRANNY GRANNY PLEASE COMB MY HAIR

Granny Granny
please comb my hair
you always take your time
you always take such care

You put me to sit on a cushion
between your knees
you rub a little coconut oil
parting gentle as a breeze

Mummy Mummy
she's always in a hurry – hurry
rush
she pulls my hair
sometimes she tugs

But Granny
you have all the time in the world
and when you're finished
you always turn my head and say
"Now who's a nice girl."

A. A. MILNE (1882–1956)

DISOBEDIENCE

James James
Morrison Morrison
Weatherby George Dupree
Took great
Care of his Mother,
Though he was only three.
James James
Said to his Mother,
'Mother,' he said, said he;
'You must never go down to the end of the town,
    if you don't go down with me.'

James James
Morrison's Mother
Put on a golden gown,
James James
Morrison's Mother
Drove to the end of the town.
James James
Morrison's Mother
Said to herself, said she:
'I can get right down to the end of the town and be
    back in time for tea.'

King John
Put up a notice,
'LOST or STOLEN or STRAYED!
JAMES JAMES
MORRISON'S MOTHER
SEEMS TO HAVE BEEN MISLAID.
LAST SEEN
WANDERING VAGUELY:
QUITE OF HER OWN ACCORD,
SHE TRIED TO GET DOWN TO THE END OF THE
    TOWN—**FORTY SHILLINGS REWARD!**'

James James
Morrison Morrison
(Commonly known as Jim)
Told his
Other relations
Not to go blaming *him*.
James James
Said to his Mother,
'Mother,' he said, said he:
'You must *never* go down to the end of the town
without consulting me.'

James James
Morrison's Mother
Hasn't been heard of since.
King John
Said he was sorry,
So did the Queen and the Prince.
King John
(Somebody told me)
Said to a man he knew:
'If people go down to the end of the town, well,
what can *anyone* do?'

(*Now then, very softly*)
J.J.
M.M.
W. G. Du P.
Took great
C/o his M*****
Though he was only 3.
J.J.
Said to his M*****
'M*****,' he said, said he:
'You-must-never-go-down-to-the-end-of-the-town-
if-you-don't-go-down-with ME!'

LINDSAY MACRAE (1961–)

THE WORLD'S MOST POPULAR MOTHER

My mother goes all weird
When friends come round to tea
She's always nicer to the friend
Than she ever is to me

We have to eat at table
We have to wash our hands
And have grown-up conversations
About summer holiday plans

The dog stays in the garden
'case he slobbers on the guest
And Mum says something really dumb
Like 'Have you changed your vest?'

Also she puts her phone voice on
The one she thinks sounds nice
The toilet's suddenly the 'loo'
Our house becomes a 'hice'

Before you've finished eating
She'll whisk away your plate
Then get your baby photos out
The ones you really hate

She goes all hip and trendy
Asks them, 'Who're your favourite bands?'
You watch your friend in horror
Become putty in her hands

Before you even know it
Cos they think your mum's so cool
You'll be sitting down to tea each day
With half the flipping school.

JOHN HEGLEY (1953–)

MAX
(likes to be with people but people don't like to be with Max)

Max is a dog with a problem
the sort of a problem it's a job to ignore
the first time they all thought it was funny
but not anymore
Picture this scene this homeloving hound
sleeping by the fire with the family round
he wakes up and makes a little sound
little Albert gets it first
he's nearest to the ground
Albert's Mum gets wind of it
and she says open the door
and whatever we've been feeding him
I don't think we should give him no more
Max does another one like old kippers
wakes up Daddy in his fireside slippers
Daddy wakes up and says open the door
Albert says it's open Dad I did it when he did it before
then Mum says it's hard to relax with Max about
yesterday it happened while we were out in the car
and it's a small car
and Granny she was sick
she's not used to it like we are
maybe we should swap him for a budgerigar
Max is smelly
he can spoil your telly
but luckily
he's not an elephant.

RUDYARD KIPLING (1865–1936)

THE HUMP

The Camel's hump is an ugly lump
    Which well you may see at the Zoo;
But uglier yet is the hump we get
    From having too little to do.

Kiddies and grown-ups too-oo-oo,
If we haven't enough to do-oo-oo,
    We get the hump—
    Cameelious hump—
The hump that is black and blue!

We climb out of bed with a frouzly head,
    And a snarly-yarly voice.
We shiver and scowl and we grunt and we growl
    At our bath and our boots and our toys;

And there ought to be a corner for me
(And I know there is one for you)
    When we get the hump—
    Cameelious hump—
The hump that is black and blue!

The cure for this ill is not to sit still,
    Or frowst with a book by the fire;
But to take a large hoe and a shovel also,
    And dig till you gently perspire;

And then you will find that the sun and the wind,
And the Djinn of the Garden too,
    Have lifted the hump—
    The horrible hump—
The hump that is black and blue!

I get it as well as you-oo-oo—
If I haven't enough to do-oo-oo!
    We all get hump—
    Cameelious hump—
Kiddies and grown-ups too!

MICHAEL ROSEN (1954–)

DON'T

Don't do.
Don't do,
Don't do that.
Don't pull faces,
Don't tease the cat.

Don't pick your ears,
Don't be rude at school.
Who do they think I am?

Some kind of fool?

One day
they'll say
Don't put toffee in my coffee
don't pour gravy on the baby
don't put beer in his ear
don't stick your toes up his nose.

Don't put confetti on the spaghetti
and don't squash peas on your knees.

Don't put ants in your pants
don't put mustard in the custard
don't chuck jelly at the telly
and don't throw fruit at the computer
don't throw fruit at the computer.

Don't what?
Don't throw fruit at the computer.
Don't what?
Don't throw fruit at the computer.
Who do they think I am?
Some kind of fool?

JOHN HEGLEY (1953–)

BONFIRE NIGHT

the doors open
everyone comes out
everyone is ready
for fireworks
except the dog
Eddie
he is shut up in the sheddie
even out of doors they have indoor fireworks
Dad says its better to be safe than dead
the air is full of the smell of next door's fireworks
Mum says they are very good this year
this year Christopher is allowed
to help his Dad light the fireworks
he is very excited
he is very proud
he is twenty eight

MICHAEL ROSEN (1954–)

I KNOW SOMEONE WHO CAN

I know someone who can
take a mouthful of custard and blow it
down their nose.
I know someone who can
make their ears wiggle.
I know someone who can
shake their cheeks so it sounds
like ducks quacking.
I know someone who can
throw peanuts in the air and catch them
in their mouth.
I know someone who can
balance a pile of 12 2p pieces on his elbow
and snatch his elbow from under them
and catch them.
I know someone who can
bend her thumb back to touch her wrist.
I know someone who can
crack his nose.
I know someone who can
say the alphabet backwards.
I know someone who can put their hands in
their armpits and blow raspberries.
I know someone who can
wiggle her little toe.
I know someone who can
lick the bottom of her chin.
I know someone who can
slide their top lip one way
and their bottom lip the other way,
and that someone is
ME.

CHARLES CAUSLEY (1917–)

TIMOTHY WINTERS

Timothy Winters comes to school
With eyes as wide as a football pool,
Ears like bombs and teeth like splinters:
A blitz of a boy is Timothy Winters.

His belly is white, his neck is dark,
And his hair is an exclamation mark.
His clothes are enough to scare a crow
And through his britches the blue winds blow.

When teacher talks he won't hear a word
And he shoots down dead the arithmetic-bird,
He licks the patterns off his plate
And he's not even heard of the Welfare State.

Timothy Winters has bloody feet
And he lives in a house on Suez Street,
He sleeps in a sack on the kitchen floor
And they say there aren't boys like him any more.

Old Man Winters likes his beer
And his missus ran off with a bombardier,
Grandma sits in the grate with a gin
And Timothy's dosed with an aspirin.

The Welfare Worker lies awake
But the law's as tricky as a ten-foot snake,
So Timothy Winters drinks his cup
And slowly goes on growing up.

At Morning Prayers the Master helves
For children less fortunate than ourselves,
And the loudest response in the room is when
Timothy Winters roars 'Amen!'

So come one angel, come on ten:
Timothy Winters says 'Amen
Amen amen amen amen.'
Timothy Winters, Lord.
Amen.

BENJAMIN ZEPHANIAH (1958–)

FRIENDS

Funky monkey in the tree
I like it when you talk to me
What I really like the best
Is when you bang upon my chest.

Slippery snake I am your mate
When all others hesitate
I'll be there right by your side
I am known to slip and slide.

Hop along, croak croak, how ya doing frog?
No one understands our deep dialogue
People may laugh when they see us on the road
We must stick together
Monkey, snake, me, you and toad.

ADRIAN MITCHELL (1932–)

DUMB INSOLENCE

I'm big for ten years old
Maybe that's why they get at me

Teachers, parents, cops
Always getting at me

When they get at me

I don't hit em
They can do you for that

I don't swear at em
They can do you for that

I stick my hands in my pockets
And stare at them

And while I stare at them
I think about sick

They call it dumb insolence

They don't like it
But they can't do you for it

BRIAN PATTEN (1946–)

THE DAY I GOT MY FINGER STUCK UP MY NOSE

When I got my finger stuck up my nose
I went to a doctor, who said,
'Nothing like this has happened before,
We will have to chop off your head.'

'It's only my finger stuck up my nose,
It's only my finger!' I said.
'I see what it is,' the doctor replied,
'But we'll still have to chop off your head.'

He went to the cabinet and took out an axe.
I watched with considerable dread.
'But it's only my finger stuck up my nose.
It's only a finger!' I said.

'Perhaps we can yank it out with a hook
Tied to some surgical thread.
Maybe we can try that,' he replied
'Rather than chop off your head.'

'I'm never going to pick it again.
I've now learned my lesson,' I said.
'I won't stick my finger up my nose—
I'll stick it in my ear instead.'

SPIKE MILLIGAN (1918–)

THE ABC

T'was midnight in the schoolroom
And every desk was shut,
When suddenly from the alphabet
Was heard a loud 'Tut-tut!'

Said A to B, 'I don't like C;
His manners are a lack.
For all I ever see of C
Is a semi-circular back!'

'I disagree,' said D to B,
I've never found C so.
From where *I* stand, he seems to be
An uncompleted O.'

C was vexed, 'I'm much perplexed,
You criticize my shape.
I'm made like that, to help spell Cat
And Cow and Cool and Cape.'

'He's right,' said E; said F, 'Whoopee!'
Said G, ''Ip, 'ip, 'ooray!'
'You're dropping me,' roared H to G.
'Don't do it please I pray!'

'Out of my way,' LL said to K.
'I'll make poor I look ILL.'
To stop this stunt, J stood in front,
And presto! ILL was JILL.

'U know,' said V, 'that W
Is twice the age of me,
For as a Roman V is five
I'm half as young as he.'

X and Y yawned sleepily,
'Look at the time!' they said.
'Let's all get off to beddy byes.'
They did, then, 'Z-z-z.'

> *or*
> *alternative last verse*

X and Y yawned sleepily,
'Look at the time!' they said.
They all jumped in to beddy byes
And the last one in was Z!'

RICHARD EDWARDS (1949–)

THE WORD PARTY

Loving words clutch crimson roses,
Rude words sniff and pick their noses,
Sly words come dressed up as foxes,
Short words stand on cardboard boxes,
Common words tell jokes and gabble,
Complicated words play Scrabble,
Swear words stamp around and shout,
Hard words stare each other out,
Foreign words look lost and shrug,
Careless words trip on the rug,
Long words slouch with stooping shoulders,
Code words carry secret folders,
Silly words flick rubber bands,
Hyphenated words hold hands,
Strong words show off, bending metal,
Sweet words call each other 'petal',
Small words yawn and suck their thumbs
Till at last the morning comes.
Kind words give out farewell posies . . .

Snap! The dictionary closes.

ROGER MCGOUGH (1937–)

FIRST DAY AT SCHOOL

A millionbillionwillion miles from home
Waiting for the bell to go. (To go where?)
Why are they all so big, other children?
So noisy? So much at home they
must have been born in uniform.
Lived all their lives in playgrounds.
Spent the years inventing games
that don't let me in. Games
that are rough, that swallow you up.

And the railings.
All around, the railings.
Are they to keep out wolves and monsters?
Things that carry off and eat children?
Things you don't take sweets from?
Perhaps they're to stop us getting out
Running away from the lessins. Lessin.
What does a lessin look like?
Sounds small and slimy.
They keep them in glassrooms.
Whole rooms made out of glass. Imagine.

I wish I could remember my name
Mummy said it would come in useful.
Like wellies. When there's puddles.
Yellowwellies. I wish she was here.
I think my name is sewn on somewhere
Perhaps the teacher will read it for me.
Tea'cher. The one who makes the tea.

ALLAN AHLBERG (1938–)

PLEASE MRS BUTLER

Please Mrs Butler
This boy Derek Drew
Keeps copying my work, Miss.
What shall I do?

Go and sit in the hall, dear.
Go and sit in the sink.
Take your books on the roof, my lamb.
Do whatever you think.

Please Mrs Butler
This boy Derek Drew
Keeps taking my rubber, Miss.
What shall I do?

Keep it in your hand, dear.
Hide it up your vest.
Swallow it if you like, my love.
Do what you think best.

Please Mrs Butler
This boy Derek Drew
Keeps calling me rude names, Miss.
What shall I do?

Lock yourself in the cupboard, dear.
Run away to sea.
Do whatever you can, my flower.
But *don't ask me!*

ALLAN AHLBERG (1938–)

THE GRUMPY TEACHER

What shall we do with the grumpy teacher?
What shall we do with the grumpy teacher?
What shall we do with the grumpy teacher,
Early in the morning?

Hang her on a hook behind the classroom door.
Tie her up and leave her in the PE store.
Make her be with Derek Drew for evermore,
Early in the morning.

Please, Miss, we're only joking,
Don't mean to be provoking.
How come your ears are smoking?
Early in the morning.

What shall we do with the grumpy teacher?
What shall we do with the grumpy teacher?
What shall we do with the grumpy teacher,
Early in the morning?

Send him out to duty when the sleet is sleeting.
Keep him after school to take a parents' meeting.
Stand him in the hall to watch the children eating,
Early in the morning.

Please, Sir, we're only teasing,
Don't mean to be displeasing.
Help—that's our necks you're squeezing!
Early in the morning.

What shall we do with the grumpy teacher?
What shall we do with the grumpy teacher?
What shall we do with the grumpy teacher,
Early in the morning?

Tickle her toes with a hairy creature.
Leave her in the jungle where the ants can reach her.
BRING HER BACK ALIVE TO BE A CLASSROOM TEACHER!
Early—in the—morning!

JACK PRELUTSKY (1940–)

HOMEWORK! OH, HOMEWORK!

Homework! Oh, homework!
I hate you! You stink!
I wish I could wash you
away in the sink,
if only a bomb
would explode you to bits.
Homework! Oh, homework!
You're giving me fits.

I'd rather take baths
with a man-eating shark,
or wrestle a lion
alone in the dark,
eat spinach and liver.
pet ten porcupines,
than tackle the homework
my teacher assigns.

Homework! Oh, homework!
You're last on my list,
I simply can't see
why you even exist,
if you just disappeared
it would tickle me pink.
Homework! Oh, homework!
I hate you! You stink!

'There, in the night, where none can spy,
All in my hunter's camp I lie,
And play at books that I have read
Till it is time to go to bed.'

from 'The Land of Story-Books'

ROBERT LOUIS STEVENSON (1850–94)

THE LAND OF STORY-BOOKS

At evening when the lamp is lit,
Around the fire my parents sit;
They sit at home and talk and sing,
And do not play at anything.

Now, with my little gun, I crawl
All in the dark along the wall,
And follow round the forest track
Away behind the sofa back.

There, in the night, where none can spy,
All in my hunter's camp I lie,
And play at books that I have read
Till it is time to go to bed.

These are the hills, these are the woods,
These are my starry solitudes;
And there the river by whose brink
The roaring lions come to drink.

I see the others far away
As if in firelit camp they lay,
And I, like to an Indian scout,
Around their party prowled about.

So, when my nurse comes in for me,
Home I return across the sea,
And go to bed with backward looks
At my dear land of Story-books.

EUGENE FIELD (1850–95)

WYNKEN, BLYNKEN, AND NOD

Wynken, Blynken, and Nod one night
Sailed off in a wooden shoe—
Sailed on a river of crystal light,
Into a sea of dew.
'Where are you going, and what do you wish?'
The old moon asked the three.
'We have come to fish for the herring fish
That live in this beautiful sea;
Nets of silver and gold have we!'
Said Wynken,
Blynken,
And Nod.

The old moon laughed and sang a song,
As they rocked in the wooden shoe,
And the wind that sped them all night long
Ruffled the waves of dew.
The little stars were the herring fish
That lived in that beautiful sea—
'Now cast your nets wherever you wish—
Never afeard are we';
So cried the stars to the fishermen three:
Wynken,
Blynken,
And Nod.

All night long their nets they threw
To the stars in the twinkling foam—
Then down from the skies came the wooden shoe,
Bringing the fishermen home;
'Twas all so pretty a sail it seemed
As if it could not be,
And some folks thought 'twas a dream they'd dreamed
Of sailing that beautiful sea—

But I shall name you the fishermen three:
Wynken,
Blynken,
And Nod.

Wynken and Blynken are two little eyes,
And Nod is a little head,
And the wooden shoe that sailed the skies
Is the wee one's trundle-bed.
So shut your eyes while mother sings
Of wonderful sights that be,
And you shall see the beautiful things
As you rock in the misty sea,
Where the old shoe rocked the fishermen three:
Wynken,
Blynken,
And Nod.

EDWARD LEAR (1812–88)

THE JUMBLIES

They went to sea in a Sieve, they did,
   In a Sieve they went to sea:
In spite of all their friends could say,
On a winter's morn, on a stormy day,
   In a Sieve they went to sea!
And when the Sieve turned round and round,
And everyone cried, 'You'll all be drowned!'
They called aloud, 'Our Sieve ain't big,
But we don't care a button! we don't care a fig!
   In a Sieve we'll go to sea!'
   Far and few, far and few,
   Are the lands where the Jumblies live;
   Their heads are green, and their hands are blue,
   And they went to sea in a Sieve.

They sailed away in a Sieve, they did,
   In a Sieve they sailed so fast,
With only a beautiful pea-green veil
Tied with a riband by way of a sail,
   To a small tobacco-pipe mast;
And everyone said, who saw them go,
'O won't they be soon upset, you know!
For the sky is dark, and the voyage is long,
And happen what may, it's extremely wrong
   In a Sieve to sail so fast!'
   Far and few, far and few,
   Are the lands where the Jumblies live;
   Their heads are green, and their hands are blue,
   And they went to sea in a Sieve.

The water it soon came in, it did,
   The water it soon came in;
So to keep them dry, they wrapped their feet
In a pinky paper all folded neat,

93

And they fastened it down with a pin.
And they passed the night in a crockery-jar,
And each of them said, 'How wise we are!
Though the sky be dark, and the voyage be long,
Yet we never can think we were rash or wrong,
  While round in our Sieve we spin!'
  Far and few, far and few,
  Are the lands where the Jumblies live;
  Their heads are green, and their hands are blue,
  And they went to sea in a Sieve.

And all night long they sailed away;
  And when the sun went down,
They whistled and warbled a moony song
To the echoing sound of a coppery gong,
  In the shade of the mountains brown.
'O Timballoo! How happy we are,
When we live in a sieve and a crockery-jar,
And all night long in the moonlight pale,
We sail away with a pea-green sail,
  In the shade of the mountains brown!'
  Far and few, far and few,
  Are the lands where the Jumblies live;
  Their heads are green, and their hands are blue,
  And they went to sea in a Sieve.

They sailed to the Western Sea, they did,
  To a land all covered with trees,
And they bought an Owl, and a useful Cart,
And a pound of Rice, and a Cranberry Tart,
  And a hive of silvery Bees.
And they bought a Pig, and some green Jackdaws,
And a lovely Monkey with lollipop paws,
And forty bottles of Ring-Bo-Ree,

And no end of Stilton Cheese.
Far and few, far and few,
Are the lands where the Jumblies live;
Their heads are green, and their hands are blue,
And they went to sea in a Sieve.

And in twenty years they all came back,
    In twenty years or more,
And everyone said, 'How tall they've grown!
For they've been to the Lakes, and the Torrible Zone,
    And the hills of the Chankly Bore';
And they drank their health, and gave them a feast
Of dumplings made of beautiful yeast;
And everyone said, 'If we only live,
We too will go to sea in a Sieve,
    To the hills of the Chankly Bore!'
    Far and few, far and few,
    Are the lands where the Jumblies live;
    Their heads are green, and their hands are blue,
    And they went to sea in a Sieve.

EDWARD LEAR (1812–88)

THE OWL AND THE PUSSY-CAT

The Owl and the Pussy-cat went to sea
    In a beautiful pea-green boat,
They took some honey, and plenty of money,
    Wrapped up in a five-pound note.
The Owl looked up to the stars above,
    And sang to a small guitar,
'O lovely Pussy! O Pussy, my love
    What a beautiful Pussy you are,
    You are,
    You are!
    What a beautiful Pussy you are!'

Pussy said to the Owl, 'You elegant fowl!
    How charmingly sweet you sing!
O let us be married! too long we have tarried:
    But what shall we do for a ring?'
They sailed away, for a year and a day,
    To the land where the Bong-tree grows,
And there in a wood a Piggy-wig stood
    With a ring at the end of his nose,
    His nose,
    His nose,
    With a ring at the end of his nose.

'Dear Pig, are you willing to sell for one shilling
    Your ring?' Said the Piggy, 'I will.'
So they took it away, and were married next day
    By the Turkey who lives on the hill.
They dined on mince, and slices of quince,
    Which they ate with a runcible spoon;
And hand in hand, on the edge of the sand,
    They danced by the light of the moon,
    The moon,
    The moon,
    They danced by the light of the moon.

ANON

I SAW A SHIP A-SAILING

I saw a ship a-sailing,
    A-sailing on the sea,
And oh but it was laden
    With pretty things for me.

There were comfits in the cabin,
    And apples in the hold;
The sails were made of silk,
    And the masts were all of gold.

The four-and-twenty sailors,
    That stood between the decks,
Were four-and-twenty white mice
    With chains about their necks.

The captain was a duck
    With a packet on his back,
And when the ship began to move
    The captain said Quack! Quack!

E. E. CUMMINGS (1894–1962)

MAGGIE AND MILLY AND MOLLY AND MAY

maggie and milly and molly and may
went down to the beach(to play one day)

and maggie discovered a shell that sang
so sweetly she couldn't remember her troubles,and

milly befriended a stranded star
whose rays five languid fingers were;

and molly was chased by a horrible thing
which raced sideways while blowing bubbles:and

may came home with a smooth round stone
as small as a world and as large as alone.

For whatever we lose(like a you or a me)
it's always ourselves we find in the sea

JOHN FOSTER (1941–)

SAND

Sand in your fingernails
Sand between your toes
Sand in your earholes
Sand up your nose!

Sand in your sandwiches
Sand on your bananas
Sand in your bed at night
Sand in your pyjamas!

Sand in your sandals
Sand in your hair
Sand in your knickers
Sand everywhere!

ROBERT LOUIS STEVENSON (1850–94)

PIRATE STORY

Three of us afloat in the meadow by the swing,
    Three of us aboard in the basket on the lea.
Winds are in the air, they are blowing in the spring,
    And waves are on the meadows like the waves there are at sea.

Where shall we adventure, today that we're afloat,
    Wary of the weather and steering by a star?
Shall it be to Africa, a-steering of a boat,
    To Providence, or Babylon, or off to Malabar?

Hi! But here's a squadron a-rowing on the sea—
    Cattle on the meadow a-charging with a roar!
Quick, and we'll escape them, they're as mad as they can be.
    The wicket is the harbour and the garden is the shore.

ELEANOR FARJEON (1881–1965)

THE DISTANCE

Over the sounding sea,
Off the wandering sea
I smelt the smell of the distance
And longed for another existence.
Smell of pineapple, maize, and myrrh,
Parrot-feather and monkey-fur,
    Brown spice,
    Blue ice,
Fields of tobacco and tea and rice,

    And soundless snows,
    And snowy cotton,
    Otto of rose
Incense in an ivory palace,
Jungle rivers rich and rotten,
    Slumbering valleys,
    Smouldering mountains,
    Rank morasses
    And frozen fountains,
Black molasses and purple wine,
Coral and pearl and tar and brine,
The smell of panther and polar-bear
    And leopard-lair
    And mermaid-hair
Came from the four-cornered distance,
And I longed for another existence.

SHIRLEY HUGHES (1927–)

THE GRASS HOUSE

The grass house
Is my private place.
Nobody can see me
In the grass house.
Feathery plumes
Meet over my head.
Down here,
In the green, there are:
Seeds
Weeds
Stalks
Pods
And tiny little flowers.

Only the cat
And some busy, hurrying ants
Know where my grass house is.

'Belinda lived in a little white house,
With a little black kitten and a little gray mouse,
And a little yellow dog and a little red wagon,
And a realio, trulio, little pet dragon.'

from 'The Tale of Custard the Dragon'

HILAIRE BELLOC (1870–1953)

MATILDA
WHO TOLD LIES, AND WAS BURNED TO DEATH

Matilda told such Dreadful Lies,
It made one Gasp and Stretch one's Eyes;
Her Aunt, who, from her Earliest Youth,
Had kept a Strict Regard for Truth,
Attempted to Believe Matilda:
The effort very nearly killed her,
And would have done so, had not She
Discovered this Infirmity.
For once, towards the Close of Day,
Matilda, growing tired of play,
And finding she was left alone,
Went tiptoe to the Telephone
And summoned the Immediate Aid
Of London's Noble Fire-Brigade.
Within an hour the Gallant Band
Were pouring in on every hand,
From Putney, Hackney Downs, and Bow.
With Courage high and Hearts a-glow,
They galloped, roaring through the Town,
'Matilda's House is Burning Down!'
Inspired by British Cheers and Loud
Proceeding from the Frenzied Crowd,
They ran their ladders through a score
Of windows on the Ball Room Floor;
And took Peculiar Pains to Souse
The Pictures up and down the House,
Until Matilda's Aunt succeeded
In showing them they were not needed;
And even then she had to pay
To get the Men to go away!

It happened that a few Weeks later
Her Aunt was off to the Theatre
To see that Interesting Play
The Second Mrs Tanqueray.
She had refused to take her Niece
To hear this Entertaining Piece:
A Deprivation Just and Wise
To Punish her for Telling Lies.
That Night a Fire *did* break out—
You should have heard Matilda Shout!
You should have heard her Scream and Bawl,
And throw the window up and call
To People passing in the Street—
(The rapidly increasing Heat
Encouraging her to obtain
Their confidence)—but all in vain!
For every time She shouted 'Fire!'
They only answered 'Little Liar!'
And therefore when her Aunt returned,
Matilda, and the House, were Burned.

HILAIRE BELLOC (1870–1953)

JIM
WHO RAN AWAY FROM HIS NURSE, AND WAS EATEN BY A LION

There was a boy whose name was Jim;
His friends were very good to him.
They gave him tea, and cakes, and jam,
And slices of delicious ham,
And chocolate with pink inside,
And little tricycles to ride,
And read him stories through and through,
And even took him to the Zoo—
But there it was the dreadful fate
Befell him, which I now relate.

You know—at least you *ought* to know,
For I have often told you so—
That children never are allowed
To leave their nurses in a crowd;
Now this was Jim's especial foible,
He ran away when he was able,
And on this inauspicious day
He slipped his hand and ran away!
He hadn't gone a yard when—Bang!
With open jaws, a lion sprang,
And hungrily began to eat
The boy: beginning at his feet.

Now, just imagine how it feels
When first your toes and then your heels,
And then by gradual degrees,
Your shins and ankles, calves and knees,
Are slowly eaten, bit by bit.
No wonder Jim detested it!
No wonder that he shouted 'Hi!'
The honest keeper heard his cry,

Though very fat he almost ran
To help the little gentleman.
'Ponto!' he ordered as he came
(For Ponto was the lion's name),
'Ponto!' he cried, with angry frown.
'Let go, Sir! Down, Sir! Put it down!'

The lion made a sudden stop,
He let the dainty morsel drop,
And slunk reluctant to his cage,
Snarling with disappointed rage.
But when he bent him over Jim,
The honest keeper's eyes were dim.
The lion having reached his head,
The miserable boy was dead!

When Nurse informed his parents, they
Were more concerned than I can say:—
His Mother, as she dried her eyes,
Said, 'Well—it gives me no surprise,
He would not do as he was told!'
His Father, who was self-controlled,
Bade all the children round attend
To James's miserable end,
And always keep a-hold of Nurse
For fear of finding something worse.

OGDEN NASH (1902–71)

ADVENTURES OF ISABEL

Isabel met an enormous bear,
Isabel, Isabel, didn't care;
The bear was hungry, the bear was ravenous,
The bear's big mouth was cruel and cavernous.
The bear said, Isabel, glad to meet you,
How do, Isabel, now I'll eat you!
Isabel, Isabel, didn't worry,
Isabel didn't scream or scurry.
She washed her hands and she straightened her hair up,
Then Isabel quietly ate the bear up.

Once in a night as black as pitch
Isabel met a wicked old witch.
The witch's face was cross and wrinkled,
The witch's gums with teeth were sprinkled.
Ho ho, Isabel! the old witch crowed,
I'll turn you into an ugly toad!
Isabel, Isabel, didn't worry,
Isabel didn't scream or scurry,
She showed no rage and she showed no rancour,
But she turned the witch into milk and drank her.

Isabel met a hideous giant,
Isabel continued self-reliant.
The giant was hairy, the giant was horrid,
He had one eye in the middle of his forehead.
Good morning, Isabel, the giant said,
I'll grind your bones to make my bread.
Isabel, Isabel, didn't worry,
Isabel didn't scream or scurry.
She nibbled the zwieback that she always fed off,
And when it was gone, she cut the giant's head off.

Isabel met a troublesome doctor,
He punched and he poked till he really shocked her.
The doctor's talk was of coughs and chills
And the doctor's satchel bulged with pills.
The doctor said unto Isabel,
Swallow this, it will make you well.
Isabel, Isabel, didn't worry,
Isabel didn't scream or scurry.
She took those pills from the pill concocter,
And Isabel calmly cured the doctor.

ANON

POOR OLD LADY

Poor old lady, she swallowed a fly.
I don't know why she swallowed a fly.
Poor old lady, I think she'll die.

Poor old lady, she swallowed a spider.
It squirmed and wriggled and turned inside her.
She swallowed the spider to catch the fly.
I don't know why she swallowed a fly.
Poor old lady, I think she'll die.

Poor old lady, she swallowed a bird.
How absurd! She swallowed a bird.
She swallowed the bird to catch the spider,
She swallowed the spider to catch the fly.
I don't know why she swallowed a fly.
Poor old lady, I think she'll die.

Poor old lady, she swallowed a cat.
Think of that! She swallowed a cat.
She swallowed the cat to catch the bird.
She swallowed the bird to catch the spider,
She swallowed the spider to catch the fly.
I don't know why she swallowed a fly.
Poor old lady, I think she'll die.

Poor old lady, she swallowed a dog.
She went the whole hog when she swallowed the dog.
She swallowed the dog to catch the cat,
She swallowed the cat to catch the bird,
She swallowed the bird to catch the spider.
She swallowed the spider to catch the fly,
I don't know why she swallowed a fly.
Poor old lady, I think she'll die.

Poor old lady, she swallowed a cow.
I don't know how she swallowed the cow.
She swallowed the cow to catch the dog,
She swallowed the dog to catch the cat,
She swallowed the cat to catch the bird,
She swallowed the bird to catch the spider,
She swallowed the spider to catch the fly,
I don't know why she swallowed a fly.
Poor old lady, I think she'll die.

Poor old lady, she swallowed a horse.
She died, of course.

ROBERT BROWNING (1812–89)

from THE PIED PIPER OF HAMELIN

Once more he stept into the street;
   And to his lips again
Laid his long pipe of smooth straight cane;
   And ere he blew three notes (such sweet
Soft notes as yet musician's cunning
   Never gave the enraptured air)
There was a rustling that seem'd like a bustling
Of merry crowds justling at pitching and hustling,
Small feet were pattering, wooden shoes clattering,
Little hands clapping, and little tongues chattering,
And, like fowls in a farm-yard when barley is scattering,
Out came the children running.
All the little boys and girls,
With rosy cheeks and flaxen curls,
And sparkling eyes and teeth like pearls,
Tripping and skipping, ran merrily after
The wonderful music with shouting and laughter.

The Mayor was dumb, and the Council stood
As if they were changed into blocks of wood,
Unable to move a step, or cry
To the children merrily skipping by —
And could only follow with the eye
That joyous crowd at the Piper's back.
But how the Mayor was on the rack,
And the wretched Council's bosoms beat,
As the Piper turn'd from the High Street
To where the Weser roll'd its waters
Right in the way of their sons and daughters!
However, he turned from south to west,
And to Koppelberg Hill his steps address'd,
And after him the children press'd;
Great was the joy in every breast.

'He never can cross that mighty top!
He's forced to let the piping drop,
And we shall see our children stop!'
When, lo, as they reach'd the mountain's side,
A wondrous portal open'd wide,
As if a cavern was suddenly hollow'd;
And the Piper advanced and the children follow'd,
And when all were in to the very last,
The door in the mountain-side shut fast.
Did I say all? No! one was lame,
And could not dance the whole of the way,
And in after years, if you would blame
His sadness, he was used to say,
'It's dull in our town since my playmates left!
I can't forget that I'm bereft
Of all the pleasant sights they see,
Which the Piper also promised me,
For he led us, he said, to a joyous land,
Joining the town and just at hand,
Where waters gush'd and fruit trees grew,
And flowers put forth a fairer hue,
And everything was strange and new;
The sparrows were brighter than peacocks here,
And the dogs outran our fallow deer,
And honey-bees had lost their stings,
And horses were born with eagles' wings;
And just as I became assured
My lame foot would be speedily cured,
The music stopp'd, and I stood still,
And found myself outside the Hill,
Left alone against my will,
To go now limping as before,
And never hear of that country more!'

ANON
———

SING A SONG OF SIXPENCE

Sing a song of sixpence,
A pocket full of rye;
Four and twenty blackbirds,
Baked in a pie.

When the pie was opened,
The birds began to sing;
Was not that a dainty dish,
To set before the king?

The king was in his counting-house,
Counting out his money;
The queen was in the parlour,
Eating bread and honey.

The maid was in the garden,
Hanging out the clothes,
Along came a blackbird,
And snapped off her nose.

WILLIAM ALLINGHAM (1824–89)

THE FAIRIES

Up the airy mountain,
　　Down the rushy glen,
We daren't go a-hunting
　　For fear of little men;
Wee folk, good folk,
　　Trooping all together;
Green jacket, red cap,
　　And white owl's feather!

Down along the rocky shore
　　Some make their home,
They live on crispy pancakes
　　Of yellow tide-foam;
Some in the reeds
　　Of the black mountain-lake,
With frogs for their watchdogs,
　　All night awake.

High on the hill-top
　　The old King sits;
He is now so old and grey
　　He's nigh lost his wits.
With a bridge of white mist
　　Columbkill he crosses,
On his stately journeys
　　From Slieveleague to Rosses;
Or going up with music
　　On cold starry nights,
To sup with the Queen
　　Of the gay Northern Lights.

They stole little Bridget
   For seven years long;
When she came down again
   Her friends were all gone.
They took her lightly back,
   Between the night and morrow,
The thought that she was fast asleep,
   But she was dead with sorrow.
They have kept her ever since
   Deep within the lake,
On a bed of flag-leaves,
   Watching till she wake.

By the craggy hillside,
   Through the mosses bare,
They have planted thorn trees
   For pleasure, here and there.
Is any man so daring
   As dig them up in spite,
He shall find their sharpest thorns
   In his bed at night.

Up the airy mountain,
   Down the rushy glen,
We daren't go a-hunting
   For fear of little men;
Wee folk, good folk,
   Trooping all together;
Green jacket, red cap,
   And white owl's feather!

EDWARD LEAR (1812–88)

THE DONG WITH A LUMINOUS NOSE

When awful darkness and silence reign
Over the great Gromboolian plain,
    Through the long, long wintry nights;—
When the angry breakers roar
As they beat on the rocky shore;—
    When Storm-clouds brood on the towering heights
Of the Hills of the Chankly Bore:—

Then, through the vast and gloomy dark,
There moves what seems a fiery spark,
    A lonely spark with silvery rays
    Piercing the coal-black night,—
    A Meteor strange and bright:—
Hither and thither the vision strays,
    A single lurid light.

Slowly it wanders,—pauses,—creeps,—
Anon it sparkles,—flashes and leaps;
And ever as onward it gleaming goes
A light on the Bong-tree stems it throws.
And those who watch at that midnight hour
From Hall or Terrace, or lofty Tower,
Cry, as the wild light passes along,—
    'The Dong!—the Dong!
    The wandering Dong through the forest goes!
    The Dong! the Dong!
    The Dong with a luminous Nose!'

    Long years ago
    The Dong was happy and gay,
Till he fell in love with a Jumbly Girl
    Who came to those shores one day,
For the Jumblies came in a Sieve, they did,—
Landing at eve near the Zemmery Fidd

Where the Oblong Oysters grow,
  And the rocks are smooth and gray.

And all the woods and the valleys rang
With the Chorus they daily and nightly sang,—
  'Far and few, far and few,
  Are the lands where the Jumblies live;
  Their heads are green, and their hands are blue,
  And they went to sea in a Sieve.'

  Happily, happily passed those days!
  While the cheerful Jumblies staid;
  They danced in circlets all night long,
  To the plaintive pipe of the lively Dong,
  In moonlight, shine, or shade.
For day and night he was always there
By the side of the Jumbly Girl so fair,
With her sky-blue hands, and her sea-green hair.
Till the morning came of that hateful day
When the Jumblies sailed in their Sieve away,
And the Dong was left on the cruel shore
Gazing—gazing for evermore,—
Ever keeping his weary eyes on
That pea-green sail on the far horizon,—
Singing the Jumbly Chorus still
As he sate all day on the grassy hill,—
  'Far and few, far and few,
  Are the lands where the Jumblies live;
  Their heads are green, and their hands are blue,
  And they went to sea in a Sieve.'

But when the sun was low in the West,
  The Dong arose and said;—
—'What little sense I once possessed

Has quite gone out of my head!' —
And since that day he wanders still
By lake and forest, marsh and hill,
Singing — 'O somewhere, in valley or plain
Might I find my Jumbly Girl again!
For ever I'll seek by lake and shore
Till I find my Jumbly Girl once more!'

Playing a pipe with silvery squeaks,
Since then his Jumbly Girl he seeks,
And because by night he could not see,
He gathered the bark of the Twangum Tree
   On the flowery plain that grows.
   And he wove him a wondrous Nose, —
A Nose as strange as a Nose could be!
Of vast proportions and painted red,
And tied with cords to the back of his head.
   — In a hollow rounded space it ended
   With a luminous Lamp within suspended,
   All fenced about
   With a bandage stout
   To prevent the wind from blowing it out; —
   And with holes all round to send the light,
   In gleaming rays on the dismal night.

And now each night, and all night long,
Over those plains still roams the Dong;
And above the wail of the Chimp and Snipe
You may hear the squeak of his plaintive pipe
While ever he seeks, but seeks in vain
To meet with his Jumbly Girl again;
Lonely and wild — all night he goes, —
The Dong with a luminous Nose!
And all who watch at the midnight hour,

From Hall or Terrace, or lofty Tower,
Cry, as they trace the Meteor bright,
Moving along through the dreary night,—
    'This is the hour when forth he goes,
    The Dong with a luminous Nose!
    Yonder—over the plain he goes;
    He goes!
    He goes;
    The Dong with a luminous Nose!'

A. A. MILNE (1882–1956)

THE KING'S BREAKFAST

The King asked
The Queen, and
The Queen asked
The Dairymaid:
'Could we have some butter for
The Royal slice of bread?'
The Queen asked
The Dairymaid,
The Dairymaid
Said: 'Certainly,
I'll go and tell
The cow
Now
Before she goes to bed.'

The Dairymaid
She curtsied,
And went and told
The Alderney:
'Don't forget the butter for
The Royal slice of bread.'
The Alderney
Said sleepily:
'You'd better tell
His Majesty
That many people nowadays
Like marmalade
Instead.'

The Dairymaid
Said: 'Fancy!'
And went to
Her Majesty.
She curtsied to the Queen, and

She turned a little red:
'Excuse me,
Your Majesty,
For taking of
The liberty,
But marmalade is tasty, if
It's very
Thickly
Spread.'

The Queen said:
'Oh!'
And went to
His Majesty:
'Talking of the butter for
The Royal slice of bread,
Many people
Think that
Marmalade
Is nicer.
Would you like to try a little
Marmalade
Instead?'

The King said:
'Bother!'
And then he said:
'Oh, deary me!'
The King sobbed: 'Oh, deary me!'
And went back to bed.
'Nobody,'
He whimpered,
'Could call me
A fussy man;

I *only* want
A little bit
Of butter for
My bread!'

The Queen said:
'There, there!'
And went to
The Dairymaid.
The Dairymaid
Said: 'There, there!'
And went to the shed.
The cow said:
'There, there!
I didn't really
Mean it;
Here's milk for his porringer
And butter for his bread.'

The Queen took
The butter
And brought it to
His Majesty;
The King said:
'Butter, eh?'
And bounced out of bed.
'Nobody,' he said: As he kissed her Tenderly,
As he slid down
The banisters,
'Nobody,
My darling,
Could call me
A fussy man—
BUT
I do like a little bit of butter to my bread!'

OGDEN NASH (1902–71)

THE TALE OF CUSTARD THE DRAGON

Belinda lived in a little white house,
With a little black kitten and a little gray mouse,
And a little yellow dog and a little red wagon,
And a realio, trulio, little pet dragon.

Now the name of the little black kitten was Ink,
And the little gray mouse, she called her Blink,
And the little yellow dog, as sharp as Mustard,
But the dragon was a coward, and she called him Custard.

Custard the dragon had big sharp teeth,
And spikes on top of him and scales underneath,
Mouth like a fireplace, chimney for a nose,
And realio, trulio daggers on his nose.

Belinda was as brave as a barrel full of bears,
And Ink and Blink chased lions down the stairs,
Mustard was as brave as a tiger in a rage,
But Custard cried for a nice safe cage.

Belinda tickled him, she tickled him unmerciful,
Ink, Blink and Mustard, they rudely called him Percival,
They all sat laughing in the little red wagon
At the realio, trulio, cowardly dragon.

Belinda giggled till she shook the house,
And Blink said Weeck! which is giggling for a mouse,
Ink and Mustard rudely asked his age,
When Custard cried for a nice safe cage.

Suddenly, suddenly they heard a nasty sound,
And Mustard growled, and they all looked around.
Meowch! cried Ink, and Ooh! cried Belinda,
For there was a pirate, climbing in the winda.

Pistol in his left hand, pistol in his right,
And he held in his teeth a cutlass bright,
His beard was black, one leg was wood;
It was clear that the pirate meant no good.

Belinda paled, and she cried Help! Help!
But Mustard fled with a terrified yelp,
Ink trickled down to the bottom of the household,
And little mouse Blink strategically mouseholed.

But up jumped Custard, snorting like an engine,
Clashed his tail like irons in a dungeon
With a clatter and a clank and a jangling squirm
He went at the pirate like a robin at a worm.

The pirate gaped at Belinda's dragon,
And gulped some grog from his pocket flagon,
He fired two bullets, but they didn't hit,
And Custard gobbled him, every bit.

Belinda embraced him, Mustard licked him,
No one mourned for his pirate victim.
Ink and Blink in glee did gyrate
Around the dragon that ate the pyrate.

Belinda still lives in her little white house,
With her little black kitten and her little gray mouse,
And her little yellow dog and her little red wagon,
And her realio, trulio, little pet dragon.

Belinda is as brave as a barrel full of bears,
And Ink and Blink chase lions down the stairs.
Mustard is as brave as a tiger in a rage,
But Custard keeps crying for a nice safe cage.

U. A. FANTHORPE (1929–)

NOT MY BEST SIDE
(Uccello: St George and the Dragon, *The National Gallery)*

I

Not my best side, I'm afraid.
The artist didn't give me a chance to
Pose properly, and as you can see,
Poor chap, he had this obsession with
Triangles, so he left off two of my
Feet. I didn't comment at the time
(What, after all, are two feet
To a monster?) but afterwards
I was sorry for the bad publicity.
Why, I said to myself, should my conqueror
Be so ostentatiously beardless, and ride
A horse with a deformed neck and square hoofs?
Why should my victim be so
Unattractive as to be inedible,
And why should she have me literally
On a string? I don't mind dying
Ritually, since I always rise again,
But I should have liked a little more blood
To show they were taking me seriously.

II

It's hard for a girl to be sure if
She wants to be rescued. I mean, I quite
Took to the dragon. It's nice to be
Liked, if you know what I mean. He was
So nicely physical, with his claws
And lovely green skin, and that sexy tail,
And the way he looked at me,
He made me feel he was all ready to
Eat me. And any girl enjoys that.
So when this boy turned up, wearing machinery,
On a really *dangerous* horse, to be honest,

I didn't much fancy him. I mean,
What was he like underneath the hardware?
He might have acne, blackheads or even
Bad breath for all I could tell, but the dragon—
Well, you could see all his equipment
At a glance. Still, what could I do?
The dragon got himself beaten by the boy,
And a girl's got to think of her future.

III

I have diplomas in Dragon
Management and Virgin Reclamation.
My horse is the latest model, with
Automatic transmission and built-in
Obsolescence. My spear is custom-built,
And my prototype armour
Still on the secret list. You can't
Do better than me at the moment.
I'm qualified and equipped to the
Eyebrow. So why be difficult?
Don't you want to be killed and/or rescued
In the most contemporary way? Don't
You want to carry out the roles
That sociology and myth have designed for you?
Don't you realize that, by being choosy,
You are endangering job-prospects
In the spear- and horse-building industries?
What, in any case, does it matter what
You want? You're in my way.

ROALD DAHL (1916–90)

LITTLE RED RIDING HOOD AND THE WOLF

As soon as Wolf began to feel
That he would like a decent meal,
He went and knocked on Grandma's door.
When Grandma opened it, she saw
The sharp white teeth, the horrid grin,
And Wolfie said, 'May I come in?'
Poor Grandmamma was terrified,
'He's going to eat me up!' she cried.
And she was absolutely right.
He ate her up in one big bite.
But Grandmamma was small and tough,
And Wolfie wailed, 'That's not enough!
I haven't yet begun to feel
That I have had a decent meal!'
He ran around the kitchen yelping,
'I've *got* to have another helping!'
Then added with a frightful leer,
'I'm therefore going to wait right here
Till Little Miss Red Riding Hood
Comes home from walking in the wood.'
He quickly put on Grandma's clothes
(Of course he hadn't eaten those.)
He dressed himself in coat and hat.
He put on shoes and after that
He even brushed and curled his hair,
Then sat himself in Grandma's chair.
In came the little girl in red.
She stopped. She stared. And then she said,

'*What great big ears you have, Grandma.*'
'*All the better to hear you with,*' the Wolf replied.
'*What great big eyes you have, Grandma,*'
    said Little Red Riding Hood.
'*All the better to see you with,*' the Wolf replied.

He sat there watching her and smiled.
He thought, I'm going to eat this child.
Compared with her old Grandmamma
She's going to taste like caviar.

Then Little Red Riding Hood said, '*But Grandma,*
what a lovely great big furry coat you have on.'
'That's wrong!' cried Wolf. 'Have you forgot
To tell me what BIG TEETH I've got?
Ah well, no matter what you say,
I'm going to eat you anyway.'
The small girl smiles. One eyelid flickers.
She whips a pistol from her knickers.
She aims it at the creature's head
And *bang bang bang*, she shoots him dead.
A few weeks later, in the wood,
I came across Miss Riding Hood.
But what a change! No cloak of red,
No silly hood upon her head.
She said, 'Hello, and do please note
My lovely furry WOLFSKIN COAT.'

'To understand the ways
of alien beings is hard,
and I've never worked it out
why they landed in my backyard.'

from 'Aliens Stole My Underpants'

SPIKE MILLIGAN (1918–)

TEETH

English Teeth, English Teeth!
Shining in the sun
A part of British heritage
Aye, each and every one.

English Teeth, Happy Teeth!
Always having fun
Clamping down on bits of fish
And sausages half done.

English Teeth! HEROES' Teeth!
Hear them click! and clack!
Let's sing a song of praise to them—
Three Cheers for the Brown Grey and Black.

PAM AYRES (1947–)

OH, I WISH I'D LOOKED AFTER ME TEETH

Oh, I wish I'd looked after me teeth,
   And spotted the perils beneath,
All the toffees I chewed,
   And the sweet sticky food,
Oh, I wish I'd looked after me teeth.

I wish I'd been that much more willin'
   When I had more tooth there than fillin'
To give-up gobstoppers,
   From respect to me choppers.
And to buy something else with me shillin'.

When I think of the lollies I licked,
   And the liquorice allsorts I picked,
Sherbet dabs, big and little,
   All that hard peanut brittle,
My conscience gets horribly pricked.

My mother, she told me no end,
   'If you got a tooth, you got a friend.'
I was young then, and careless,
   My toothbrush was hairless,
I never had much time to spend.

Oh I showed them the toothpaste all right,
   I flashed it about late at night,
But up-and-down brushin'
   And pokin' and fussin'
Didn't seem worth the time—I could bite!

If I'd known I was paving the way
   To cavities, caps and decay,
The murder of fillin's
   Injections and drillin's,
I'd have thrown all me sherbert away.

So I lay in the old dentist's chair,
    And I gaze up his nose in despair,
And his drill it do whine,
    In these molars of mine.
'Two amalgum,' he'll say, 'for in there.'

How I laughed at my mother's false teeth,
    As they foamed in the waters beneath.
But now comes the reckonin'
    It's *me* they are beckonin'
Oh, I *wish* I'd looked after me teeth.

IAN SERRAILLIER (1912–94)

THE TICKLE RHYME

'Who's that tickling my back?' said the wall.
'Me,' said a small
Caterpillar. 'I'm learning
To crawl.'

SPIKE MILLIGAN (1918–)

ON THE NING NANG NONG

On the Ning Nang Nong
Where the Cows go Bong!
And the Monkeys all say Boo!
There's a Nong Nang Ning
Where the trees go Ping!
And the tea pots Jibber Jabber Joo.
On the Nong Ning Nang
All the mice go Clang!
And you just can't catch 'em when they do!
So it's Ning Nang Nong!
Cows go Bong!
Nong Nang Ning!
Trees go Ping!
Nong Ning Nang!
The mice go Clang!

What a noisy place to belong,
Is the Ning Nang Ning Nang Nong!!

BRIAN MOSES (1950–)

ALIENS STOLE MY UNDERPANTS

To understand the ways
of alien beings is hard,
and I've never worked it out
why they landed in my backyard.

And I've always wondered why
on their journey from the stars,
these aliens stole my underpants
and took them back to Mars.

They came on a Monday night
when the weekend wash had been done,
pegged out on the line
to be dried by the morning sun.

Mrs Driver from next door
was a witness at the scene
when aliens snatched my underpants—
I'm glad that they were clean!

It seems they were quite choosy
as nothing else was taken.
Do aliens wear underpants
or were they just mistaken?

I think I have a theory
as to what they wanted them for,
they needed to block off a draught
blowing in through the spacecraft door.

Or maybe some Mars museum
wanted items brought back from Space.
Just think, my pair of Y-fronts
displayed in their own glass case.

And on the label beneath
would be written where they got 'em
and how such funny underwear
once covered an Earthling's bottom!

WENDY COPE (1945–)

THE JOY OF SOCKS

Nice warm socks,
Nice warm socks—
We should celebrate them.
Ask a toe!
Toes all know
It's hard to overrate them.

Toes say, 'Please
Don't let us freeze
Till we're numb and white.
Summer's gone—
Put them on!
Wear them day and night!'

Nice warm socks,
Nice warm socks—
Who would dare to mock them?
Take good care
Of every pair
And never, ever knock them.

EDWARD LEAR (1812–88)

THE POBBLE WHO HAS NO TOES

The Pobble who has no toes
    Had once as many as we;
When they said, 'Some day you may lose them all;'—
He replied,—'Fish fiddle de-dee!'
And his Aunt Jobiska made him drink,
Lavender water tinged with pink,
For she said, 'The World in general knows
There's nothing so good for a Pobble's toes!'
The Pobble who has no toes,
    Swam across the Bristol Channel;
But before he set out he wrapped his nose
    In a piece of scarlet flannel.
For his Aunt Jobiska said, 'No harm
Can come to his toes if his nose is warm;
And it's perfectly known that a Pobble's toes
Are safe,—provided he minds his nose.'
The Pobble swam fast and well,
    And when boats or ships came near him
He tinkledy-binkledy-winkled a bell,
    So that all the world could hear him.
And all the Sailors and Admirals cried,
When they saw him nearing the further side,—
'He has gone to fish, for his Aunt Jobiska's
Runcible Cat with crimson whiskers!'
But before he touched the shore,
    The shore of the Bristol Channel,
A sea-green Porpoise carried away
    His wrapper of scarlet flannel.
And when he came to observe his feet,
Formerly garnished with toes so neat,
His face at once became forlorn
On perceiving that all his toes were gone!
And nobody ever knew
    From that dark day to the present,

Whoso had taken the Pobble's toes,
    In a manner far from pleasant.
Whether the shrimps or crawfish gray,
Or crafty Mermaids stole them away—
Nobody knew; and nobody knows
How the Pobble was robbed of his twice five toes!
The Pobble who has no toes
    Was placed in a friendly Bark,
And they rowed him back, and carried him up,
    To his Aunt Jobiska's Park.
And she made him a feast at his earnest wish
Of eggs and buttercups fried with fish;—
And she said,—'It's a fact the whole world knows,
That Pobbles are happier without their toes.'

LEWIS CARROLL (1832–98)

JABBERWOCKY

'Twas brillig, and the slithy toves
   Did gyre and gimble in the wabe:
All mimsy were the borogoves,
   And the mome raths outgrabe.

'Beware the Jabberwock, my son!
   The jaws that bite, the claws that catch!
Beware the Jubjub bird, and shun
   The frumious Bandersnatch!'

He took his vorpal sword in hand:
   Long time the manxome foe he sought—
So rested he by the Tumtum tree,
   And stood awhile in thought.

And as in uffish thought he stood,
   The Jabberwock, with eyes of flame,
Came whiffling through the tulgey wood,
   And burbled as it came!

One, two! One, two! And through and through
   The vorpal blade went snicker-snack!
He left it dead, and with its head
   He went galumphing back.

'And hast thou slain the Jabberwock?
   Come to my arms, my beamish boy!
O frabjous day! Callooh! Callay!'
   He chortled in his joy.

'Twas brillig, and the slithy toves
   Did gyre and gimble in the wabe:
All mimsy were the borogoves,
   And the mome raths outgrabe.

EDWIN MORGAN (1920–)

THE COMPUTER'S FIRST CHRISTMAS CARD

jollymerry
hollyberry
jollyberry
merryholly
happyjolly
jollyjelly
jellybelly
bellymerry
hollyheppy
jollyMolly
marryJerry
merryHarry
happyBarry
heppyJarry
boppyheppy
berryjorry
jorryjolly
moppyjelly
Mollymerry
Jerryjolly
bellyboppy
jorryhoppy
hollymoppy
Barrymerry
Jarryhappy
happyboppy
boppyjolly
jollymerry
merrymerry
merrymerry
merryChris
ammerryasa
Chrismerry
asMERRYCHR
YSANTHEMUM

'The night will never stay,
The night will still go by,
Though with a million stars
You pin it to the sky'

from 'The Night Will Never Stay'

SYLVIA PLATH (1932–63)

---

from THE BED BOOK

Beds come in all sizes—
Single or double,
Cot-size or cradle,
King-size or trundle.

Most Beds are Beds
For sleeping or resting,
But the *best* Beds are much
More interesting!

Not just a white little
Tucked-in-tight little
Nighty-night little
Turn-out-the-light little
Bed—

Instead
A Bed for Fishing,
A Bed for Cats,
A Bed for a Troupe of
Acrobats.

The *right* sort of Bed
(If you see what I mean)
Is a Bed that might
Be a Submarine

Nosing through water
Clear and green,
Silver and glittery
As a sardine

Or a Jet-Propelled Bed
For visiting Mars
With mosquito nets
For the shooting stars . . .

ELEANOR FARJEON (1881–1965)

THE SOUNDS IN THE EVENING

The sounds in the evening
Go all through the house,
The click of the clock
And the pick of the mouse,
The footsteps of people
Upon the top floor,
The skirts of my mother
That brush by my door,
The crick in the boards,
And the creak of the chairs,
The fluttering murmurs
Outside on the stairs,
The ring at the bell,
The arrival of guests,
The laugh of my father
At one of his jests,
The clashing of dishes
As dinner goes in,
The babble of voices
That distance makes thin,
The mewings of cats
That seem just by my ear,
The hooting of owls
That can never seem near,
The queer little noises
That no one explains—
Till the moon through the slats
Of my window-blind rains,
And the world of my eyes
And my ears melts like steam
As I find in my pillow
The world of my dream.

GRACE NICHOLS (1950–)

I LIKE TO STAY UP

I like to stay up
and listen
when big people talking
jumbie stories

I does feel
so tingly and excited
inside me

But when my mother say
'Girl, time for bed'

Then is when
I does feel a dread

Then is when
I does jump into me bed

Then is when
I does cover up
from me feet to me head

Then is when
I does wish I didn't listen
to no stupid jumbie story

Then is when
I does wish I did read
me book instead.

WALTER DE LA MARE (1873–1956)

SOME ONE

Some one came knocking
　　At my wee, small door;
Some one came knocking,
　　I'm sure—sure—sure;
I listened, I opened,
　　I looked to left and right,
But nought there was a-stirring
　　In the still dark night;
Only the busy beetle
　　Tap-tapping in the wall,
Only from the forest
　　The screech-owl's call,
Only the cricket whistling
　　While the dewdrops fall,
So I know not who came knocking,
　　At all, at all, at all.

MICHAEL DUGAN (1947–)

NIGHTENING

When you wake up at night
And it's dark and frightening,
Climb out of bed
And turn on the lightening.

ELEANOR FARJEON (1881–1965)

THE NIGHT WILL NEVER STAY

The night will never stay,
    The night will still go by,
Though with a million stars
    You pin it to the sky,
Though you bind it with the blowing wind
    And buckle it with the moon,
The night will slip away
    Like sorrow or a tune.

ADRIAN HENRI (1932–2000)
───────────────

KATE'S UNICORN

I saw a unicorn in the garden,
I did, the other night,
admittedly it was twelve o'clock
but the moon was really bright

I got up to go to the toilet
looked out of the window to see
a gleaming white shape in the shadows
I'll swear that it looked up at me

It nibbled on the azaleas,
sniffed at the lilacs and then
started in on Dad's dahlias
and looked up at the window again

I tried to call downstairs quietly
but they couldn't hear for the TV
So I tiptoed to the back door
but he'd gone: there was nothing to see

Next day I looked in the garden
there were hoofmarks on the flowerbeds,
some broken lilac-branches
and withered dahlia heads

Each night now I look through the window
when the moon is full and round
did I see something move in the shadows,
hear a distant, neighing sound?

Mum and Dad and the others all tell me
I'm the biggest liar ever born
But I know that he'll come back to see me soon,
my midnight unicorn.

JANE TAYLOR (1783–1824)

THE STAR

Twinkle, twinkle, little star,
How I wonder what you are!
Up above the world so high,
Like a diamond in the sky.

When the blazing sun is gone,
When he nothing shines upon,
Then you show your little light,
Twinkle, twinkle, all the night.

Then the traveller in the dark,
Thanks you for your tiny spark,
He could not see which way to go,
If you did not twinkle so.

In the dark blue sky you keep,
And often through my curtains peep,
For you never shut your eye,
Till the sun is in the sky.

As your bright and tiny spark,
Lights the traveller in the dark —
Though I know now what you are,
Twinkle, twinkle, little star.

*'What a shame you can't buy
tokens of time, save them up
and lengthen the good days'*

from 'Days'

GEORGE MACKAY BROWN (1921–96)

A CHILD'S CALENDAR

No visitors in January.
A snowman smokes a cold pipe in the yard.

They stand about like ancient women,
The February hills.
They have seen many a coming and going, the hills.

In March, Moorfea is littered
With knock-kneed lambs.

Daffodils at the door in April,
Three shawled Marys.
A lark splurges in galilees of sky.

And in May
Peatmen strike the bog with spades,
Summoning black fire.

The June bee
Bumps in the pane with a heavy bag of plunder.

Strangers swarm in July
With cameras, binoculars, bird books.

He thumped the crag in August,
A blind blue whale.

September crofts get wrecked in blond surges.
They struggle, the harvesters,
They drag loaf and ale-kirn into winter.

In October the fishmonger
Argues, pleads, threatens at the shore.

Nothing in November
But tinkers at the door, keening, with cans.

Some December midnight
Christ, Lord, lie warm in our byre.
Here are stars, an ox, poverty enough.

JAMES REEVES (1909–78)

SLOWLY

Slowly the tide creeps up the sand,
Slowly the shadows cross the land.
Slowly the cart-horse pulls his mile,
Slowly the old man mounts the stile.

Slowly the hands move round the clock,
Slowly the dew dries on the dock.
Slow is the snail—but slowest of all
The green moss spreads on the old brick wall.

E. NESBIT (1858–1924)

CHILD'S SONG IN SPRING

The silver birch is a dainty lady,
  She wears a satin gown;
The elm tree makes the old churchyard shady,
  She will not live in town.

The English oak is a sturdy fellow,
  He gets his green coat late;
The willow is smart in a suit of yellow,
  While brown the beech trees wait.

Such a gay green gown God gives the larches—
  As green as He is good!
The hazels hold up their arms for arches,
  When Spring rides through the wood.

The chestnut's proud and the lilac's pretty,
  The poplar's gentle and tall,
But the plane tree's kind to the poor dull city—
  I love him best of all!

ROBERT LOUIS STEVENSON (1850–94)

BED IN SUMMER

In winter I get up at night
And dress by yellow candle-light.
In summer, quite the other way,
I have to go to bed by day.

I have to go to bed and see
The birds still hopping on the tree,
Or hear the grown up people's feet
Still going past me in the street.

And does it not seem hard to you,
When all the sky is clear and blue,
And I should like so much to play,
To have to go to bed by day?

BRIAN MOSES (1950–)

DAYS

Days fly by on holidays,
they escape like birds
released from cages.
What a shame you can't buy
tokens of time, save them up
and lengthen the good days,
or maybe you could tear out time
from days that drag, then pay it back
on holidays, wild days,
days you wish would last forever.
You could wear these days with pride,
fasten them like poppies to your coat,
or keep them in a tin, like sweets,
a confection of days
to be held on the tongue
and tasted, now and then.

THOMAS HOOD (1799–1845)

IN THE SUMMER

In the summer when I go to bed
The sun still streaming overhead
My bed becomes so small and hot
With sheets and pillow in a knot,
And then I lie and try to see
The things I'd really like to be.

I think I'd be a glossy cat
A little plum, but not too fat.
I'd never touch a bird or mouse
I'm much too busy round the house.

And then a fierce and hungry hound
The king of dogs for miles around;
I'd chase the postman just for fun
To see how quickly he could run.

Perhaps I'd be a crocodile
Within the marshes of the Nile
And paddle in the river-bed
With dripping mud-caps on my head.

Or maybe next a mountain goat
With shaggy whiskers at my throat,
Leaping streams and jumping rocks
In stripey pink and purple socks.

Or else I'd be a polar bear
And on an iceberg make my lair;
I'd keep a shop in Baffin Sound
To sell icebergs by the pound.

And then I'd be a wise old frog
Squatting on a sunken log,
I'd teach the fishes lots of games
And how to read and write their names.

An Indian lion then I'd be
And lounge about on my settee;
I'd feed on nothing but bananas
And spend all day in my pyjamas.

I'd like to be a tall giraffe
making lots of people laugh,
I'd do a tap dance in the street
with little bells upon my feet.

And then I'd be a foxy fox
Streaking through the hollyhocks,
Horse or hound would ne'er catch me
I'm a master of disguise, you see.

I think I'd be a chimpanzee
With musical ability,
I'd play a silver clarinet
Or form a Monkey String Quartet.

And then a snake with scales of gold
Guarding hoards of wealth untold,
No thief would dare to steal a pin—
But friends of mine I would let in.

But then before I really know
Just what I'd be or where I'd go
My bed becomes so wide and deep
And all my thoughts are fast asleep.

A. A. MILNE (1882–1956)

WAITING AT THE WINDOW

These are my two drops of rain
Waiting on the window-pane.

I am waiting here to see
Which the winning one will be.

Both of them have different names.
One is John and one is James.

All the best and all the worst
Comes from which one of them is first.

James had just begun to ooze.
He's the one I want to lose.

John is waiting to begin.
He's the one I want to win.

James is going slowly on.
Something sort of sticks to John.

John is moving off at last.
James is going pretty fast.

John is rushing down the pane.
James is going slow again.

James has met a sort of smear.
John is getting very near.

Is he going fast enough?
(James has found a piece of fluff.)

John has hurried quickly by.
(James was talking to a fly.)

John is there, and John has won!
Look! I told you! Here's the sun!

SPIKE MILLIGAN (1918–)

RAIN

There are holes in the sky
  Where the rain gets in,
But they're ever so small
  That's why rain is thin.

ROBERT LOUIS STEVENSON (1850–94)

WINDY NIGHTS

Whenever the moon and stars are set,
  Whenever the wind is high,
All night long in the dark and wet,
  A man goes riding by.
Late in the night when the fires are out,
Why does he gallop and gallop about?

Whenever the trees are crying aloud,
  And ships are tossed at sea,
By, on the highway, low and loud,
  By at the gallop goes he.
By at the gallop he goes, and then
By he comes back at the gallop again.

DOROTHY WORDSWORTH (1771–1855)

ADDRESS TO A CHILD DURING A BOISTEROUS WINTE EVENING

What way does the Wind come? What way does he go?
He rides over the water, and over the snow,
Through wood, and through vale; and o'er rocky height,
Which the goat cannot climb, takes his sounding flight;
He tosses about in every bare tree,
As, if you look up, you plainly may see;
But how he will come, and whither he goes,
There's never a scholar in England knows.

He will suddenly stop in a cunning nook,
And rings a sharp 'larum; but, if you should look,
There's nothing to see but a cushion of snow
Round as a pillow, and whiter than milk,
And softer than if it were covered with silk.
Sometimes he'll hide in the cave of a rock,
Then whistle as shrill as the buzzard cock.
Yet seek him—and what shall you find in his place?
Nothing but silence and empty space;
Save, in a corner, a heap of dry leaves,
That he's left, for a bed, to beggars or thieves!

As soon as 'tis daylight, tomorrow with me
You shall go to the orchard, and then you will see
That he has been there, and made a great rout,
And cracked the branches, and strewn them about:
Heaven grant that he spare but that one upright twig
That looked up at the sky so proud and big
All last summer, as well you know,
Studded with apples, a beautiful show!

Hark! over the roof he makes a pause,
And growls as if he would fix his claws
Right in the slates, and with a huge rattle
Drive them down, like men in battle.
But let him range round; he does us no harm,
We build up the fire, we're snug and warm;
Untouched by his breath, see the candle shines bright,
And burns with a clear and steady light.
Books have we to read—but that half-stifled knell,
Alas! 'tis the sound of the eight o'clock bell.

Come, now we'll to bed! and when we are there
He may work his own will, and what shall we care?
He may knock at the door—we'll not let him in;
May drive at the windows—we'll laugh at his din.
Let him seek his own home, wherever it be:
Here's a cosy warm house for Edward and me.

WILLIAM HOWITT (1792–1879)

THE WIND IN A FROLIC

The wind one morning sprung up from sleep,
Saying, 'Now for a frolic! now for a leap!
Now for a mad-cap, galloping chase!
I'll make a commotion in every place!'
So it swept with a bustle right through a great town,
Creaking the signs, and scattering down
Shutters; and whisking, with merciless squalls,
Old women's bonnets and gingerbread stalls.
There never was heard a much lustier shout,
As the apples and oranges trundled about;
And the urchins, that stand with their thievish eyes
For ever on watch, ran off each with a prize.

Then away to the field it went blustering and humming,
And the cattle all wondered whatever was coming;
It plucked by their tails the grave, matronly cows,
And tossed the colts' manes all about their brows,
Till, offended at such a familiar salute,
They all turned their backs, and stood sullenly mute.
So on it went, capering and playing its pranks:
Whistling with reeds on the broad river's banks;
Puffing the birds as they sat on the spray,
Or the traveller grave on the king's highway.
It was not too nice to hustle the bags
Of the beggar, and flutter his dirty rags:
'Twas so bold, that it feared not to play its joke
With the doctor's wig, or the gentleman's cloak.
Through the forest it roared, and cried gaily, 'Now,
You sturdy old oaks, I'll make you bow!'
And it made them bow without more ado,
Or it cracked their great branches through and through.

Then it rushed like a monster on cottage and farm,
Striking their dwellers with sudden alarm;
And they ran out like bees in a midsummer swarm.
There were dames with their 'kerchiefs tied over their caps,
To see if their poultry were free from mishaps;
The turkeys they gobbled, the geese screamed aloud,
And the hens crept to roost in a terrified crowd;
There was rearing of ladders, and logs laying on
Where the thatch from the roof threatened soon to be gone.

But the wind had passed on, and had met in a lane,
With a schoolboy, who panted and struggled in vain;
For it tossed him, and twirled him, then passed, and he stood,
With his hat in a pool, and his shoe in the mud.

There was a poor man, hoary and old,
Cutting the heath on the open wold —
The strokes of his bill were faint and few,
Ere this frolicsome wind upon him blew;
But behind him, before him, about him it came,
And the breath seemed gone from his feeble frame;
So he sat him down with a muttering tone,
Saying, 'Plague on the wind! was the like ever known?
But nowadays every wind that blows
Tells one how weak an old man grows!'

But away went the wind in its holiday glee;
And now it was far on the billowy sea,
And the lordly ships felt its staggering blow,
And the little boats darted to and fro,
But lo! it was night, and it sank to rest,
On the sea-bird's rock, in the gleaming west,
Laughing to think, in its fearful fun,
How little of mischief it had done.

ROBERT FROST (1874–1963)

STOPPING BY WOODS ON A SNOWY EVENING

Whose woods these are I think I know.
His house is in the village, though;
He will not see me stopping here
To watch his woods fill up with snow.

My little horse must think it queer
To stop without a farmhouse near
Between the woods and frozen lake
The darkest evening of the year.

He gives his harness bells a shake
To ask if there is some mistake.
The only other sound's the sweep
Of easy wind and downy flake.

The woods are lovely, dark, and deep,
But I have promises to keep,
And miles to go before I sleep,
And miles to go before I sleep.

A. A. MILNE (1882–1956)

THE MORE IT SNOWS

The more it
SNOWS-tiddely-pom,
The more it
GOES-tiddely-pom,
The more it
GOES-tiddely-pom,
On
Snowing.

And nobody
KNOWS-tiddely-pom,
How cold my
TOES-tiddely-pom,
How cold my
TOES-tiddely-pom,
Are
Growing.

ACKNOWLEDGEMENTS

— ◇ —

The publishers would like to acknowledge the following for permission to reproduce copyright material. Every effort has been made to trace copyright holders but in a few cases this has proved impossible. The publishers would be interested to hear from any copyright holders not here acknowledged.

13. 'The Bear' from *Animal Alphabet* by Richard Digance (Michael Joseph, 1980). Copyright © Richard Digance, 1980. Reprinted by permission of Penguin Books.
16. 'Mr Mistoffelees' from *Old Possum's Book of Practical Cats* by T.S. Eliot. Reprinted by permission of Faber and Faber Ltd.
18. 'The African Lion' by A.E. Housman is reprinted by permission of the Society of Authors as the Literary Representative of the Estate of A.E. Housman.
19. 'The Cats' Protection League' from *Bad Bad Cats* by Roger McGough (Puffin, 1997). Reprinted by permission of PFD on behalf of Roger McGough. © Roger McGough.
22, 33, 72. 'I Saw a Jolly Hunter', 'Out in the Desert', 'Timothy Winters' from *Collected Poems 1951–2000* by Charles Causley, published by Macmillan. Reprinted by permission of David Higham Associates.
23. 'Don't Call Alligator Long-Mouth Till You Cross River' from *Say It Again Granny* by John Agard published by Bodley Head. Used by permission of The Random House Group Limited.
26, 77, 141, 145, 178. 'Today I Saw a Little Worm', 'The ABC', 'Teeth', 'On the Ning Nang Nong', 'Rain' from *Silly Verse for Kids* by Spike Milligan, published by Puffin Books (1968). Reprinted by permission of Spike Milligan Productions Ltd.
24, 27, 107, 109. 'The Microbe', 'The Frog', 'Matilda', 'Jim' from *Complete Verse* by Hilaire Belloc, published by Random House UK Ltd. Reprinted by permission of PFD on behalf of: *The Estate of Hilaire Belloc*. © Estate of Hilaire Belloc.
28, 37. 'Song of Mr Toad', 'Ducks' Ditty' from *The Wind in the Willows* by Kenneth Grahame copyright The University Chest, Oxford, reproduced by permission of Curtis Brown Ltd.
29. 'Triolet' from *The Collected Poems of G.K. Chesterton* is reprinted by permission of A.P. Watt on behalf of The Royal Literary Fund.
169. 'Slowly' by James Reeves © James Reeves from *Complete Poems for Children* (Heinemann). Reprinted by permission of the James Reeves Estate.
41. 'The Hippopotamus Song'. Words by Michael Flanders. Music by Donald Swann. © 1952 Chappell Music ltd, London W6 8BS. Lyrics reproduced by permission of IMP Ltd. All rights reserved.
45, 176. 'Us Two', 'Waiting at the Window' from *Now We Are Six* © A.A. Milne. Copyright under the Berne Convention. Published by Methuen, an imprint of Egmont Children's Books Limited, London and used with permission.
47, 61, 126. 'Happiness', 'Disobedience', 'The King's Breakfast' from *When We*

Were Very Young © A.A. Milne. Copyright under the Berne Convention. Published by Methuen, an imprint of Egmont Children's Books Limited, London and used with permission.

53. 'Down Vith Children! Do Them In!' from *The Witches* by Roald Dahl, published by Jonathan Cape and Penguin Books. Reprinted by permission of David Higham Associates.

55. 'The Trouble with My Sister' from *Gargling with Jelly* by Brian Patten (1985). Copyright © Brian Patten, 1985. Reprinted by permission of Penguin Books.

57. 'My Other Granny' from *Meet My Folks* by Ted Hughes. Reprinted by permission of Faber and Faber Ltd.

60. 'Granny Granny Please Comb My Hair' from *I Like That Stuff* by Grace Nichols. Reproduced with permission of Curtis Brown London on behalf of Grace Nichols. © Grace Nichols, 1988.

63. 'The World's Most Popular Mother' from *How to Avoid Kissing Your Parents in Public* by Lindsay Macrae (Puffin, 2000). Copyright © Lindsay Macrae, 2000.

65, 70. 'Max', 'Bonfire Night' from *Glad to Wear Glasses* by John Hegley, published by Andre Deutsch Ltd, 1991. Reprinted by permission of PFD on behalf of John Hegley. © John Hegley, 1991.

66. 'The Hump' from *Rudyard Kipling's Verse: Definitive Edition* is reprinted by permission of A.P. Watt on behalf of The National Trust for Places of Historical Interest or Natural Beauty.

68. 'Don't' from *Don't Put Mustard in the Custard* by Michael Rosen, published by Scholastic Books. Reprinted by permission of PFD on behalf of Michael Rosen. © Michael Rosen.

71. 'I Know Someone Who Can' from *Quick Let's Get Out of Here* by Michael Rosen, published by Andre Deutsch Children's Books. Reprinted by permission of PFD on behalf of Michael Rosen. © Michael Rosen.

74. 'Friends', 'Talking Turkeys!!' from *Talking Turkeys* by Benjamin Zephaniah (Viking, 1994). © Benjamin Zephaniah, 1994. Reproduced by permission of Penguin Books.

75. 'Dumb Insolence' from *Balloon Lagoon and the Magic Islands of Poetry* by Adrian Mitchell, published by Orchard Books. Reprinted by permission of PFD on behalf of Adrian Mitchell. Educational Health Warning! Adrian Mitchell asks that none of his poems are used in connection to any examination whatsoever. © Adrian Mitchell.

76. 'The Day I Got My Finger Stuck Up My Nose' from *Juggling with Gerbils* by Brian Patten. Copyright © Brian Patten, 2000. Reproduced by permission of the author c/o Rogers, Coleridge and White, 20 Powis Mews, London W11 1JN.

79. 'The Word Party' from *The Word Party* by Richard Edwards (Lutterworth Press, 1986). Reprinted by permission of The Lutterworth Press.

80. 'First Day at School' from *In the Glass Room* by Roger McGough, published by Jonathan Cape. Reprinted by permission of PFD on behalf of Roger McGough. © Roger McGough.

82. 'Please Mrs Butler' from *Please Mrs Butler* by Allan Ahlberg (Kestrel, 1983). Copyright © Allan Ahlberg, 1983.

83. 'The Grumpy Teacher' from *Heard It in the Playground* by Allan Ahlberg,

(Viking,1989). Copyright © Allan Ahlberg. Reprinted by permission of Penguin Books.
85. 'Homework! Oh Homework!' from *New Kid on the Block* © Jack Prelutsky 1984.
Published in the UK by Heinemann Young Books, an imprint of Egmont Children's
Books Limited, London and used with permission.
99. 'maggie and milly and molly and may' is reprinted from *The Complete Poems
1904–1962*, by E.E. Cummings, edited by George J. Firmage, by permission of W.W.
Norton & Company. Copyright © 1991 by the Trustees for the E.E. Cummings Trust
and George James Firmage.
100. 'Sand' © 1991 John Foster from *Four O'Clock Friday* (Oxford University
Press), included by permission of the author.
102. 'The Distance' from *Silver Sand and Snow* by Eleanor Farjeon, published by
Michael Joseph. Reprinted by permission of David Higham Associates.
103. 'The Grass House' from *Out and About* copyright © Shirley Hughes, 1988.
Reprinted by permission of Walker Books Ltd, London.
112, 129. 'Adventures of Isabel', 'The Tale of Custard the Dragon' by Ogden Nash
are reprinted by permission of Andre Deutsch.
133. 'Not My Best Side' from *Side Effects* (1978) by U.A. Fanthorpe. Copyright U.A.
Fanthorpe. Reproduced by permission of Peterloo Poets.
135. 'Little Red Riding Hood and the Wolf' from *Revolting Rhymes* by Roald Dahl
published by Jonathan Cape. Used by permission of The Random House Group
Limited.
142. 'Oh, I Wish I'd Looked After My Teeth' from *The Works* by Pam Ayres (BBC
Wordwide). Copyright © Pam Ayres 1992. Reprinted by permission of Sheil Land
Associates Ltd.
144. 'The Tickle Rhyme' from *The Monster Horse* by Ian Serraillier (Oxford
University Press, 1950). Reprinted by permission of Anne Serraillier.
146. 'Aliens Stole My Underpants' from *The Works* by Brian Moses. Copyright ©
Brian Moses. Reproduced by permission of Macmillan Children's Books, London.
148. 'The Joy of Socks' by Wendy Cope is reprinted by permission of the author.
152. Carcanet Press for 'The Computer's First Christmas Card' from *Collected Poems*
(1990) by Edwin Morgan.
155. Extract from *The Bed Book* by Sylvia Plath. Reprinted by permission of Faber
and Faber Ltd.
157, 161. 'The Sounds in the Evening', 'The Night Will Never Stay' from *Blackbird
Has Spoken* by Eleanor Farjeon, published by Macmillan. Reprinted by permission of
David Higham Associates.
158. 'I Like to Stay Up' from *Come Into My Tropical Garden* by Grace Nichols (A &
C Black 1988). Reproduced with permission of Curtis Brown London, on behalf of
Grace Nichols. © Grace Nichols, 1988.
159. 'Some One' from *The Complete Poems of Walter de la Mare* (1969) is reprinted
by permission of the Literary Trustees of Walter de la Mare and the Society of
Authors as their representative.
160. 'Nightening' from *Flocks, Socks and Other Shocks* by Michael Dugan © Michael
Dugan, 1987. Published by Penguin Books Australia.
163. 'Kate's Unicorn' by Adrian Henri. Copyright © Adrian Henri. Reproduced by
permission of the author c/o Rogers, Coleridge and White, 20 Powis Mews, London
W11 1JN.

167. 'A Child's Calendar' from *Selected Poems* by George Mackay Brown. Reprinted by permission of John Murray (Publishers) Ltd.
172. 'Days' from *Barking Back at Dogs* by Brian Moses. Copyright © Brian Moses. Reproduced by permission of Macmillan Children's Books, London.
184. 'Stopping by Woods on a Snowy Evening' from *The Poetry of Robert Frost*, edited by Edward Connery Lathem, the Estate of Robert Frost and Jonathan Cape as publisher. Used by permission of The Random House Group Limited.
185. 'The More It Snows' from *The House at Pooh Corner* © A.A. Milne. Copyright under the Berne Convention. Published by Methuen, an imprint of Egmont Children's Books Limited, London and used with permission.

INDEX OF POETS' NAMES

— ◇ —